The Challenge of Making Cities Liveable in East Asia

THE CHALLENGE OF MAKING CITIES LIVEABLE IN EAST ASIA

Editors

LYE Liang Fook
John WONG
East Asian Institute, NUS, Singapore

World Scientific

NEW JERSEY • LONDON • SINGAPORE • BEIJING • SHANGHAI • HONG KONG • TAIPEI • CHENNAI • TOKYO

Published by

World Scientific Publishing Co. Pte. Ltd.
5 Toh Tuck Link, Singapore 596224
USA office: 27 Warren Street, Suite 401-402, Hackensack, NJ 07601
UK office: 57 Shelton Street, Covent Garden, London WC2H 9HE

Library of Congress Cataloging-in-Publication Data
Names: Lye, Liang Fook, editor. | Wong, John, 1939– editor.
Title: The challenge of making cities liveable in East Asia / edited by Liang Fook Lye, John Wong.
Description: Singapore : World Scientific, [2016]
Identifiers: LCCN 2016008380 | ISBN 9789813109735
Subjects: LCSH: Sustainable urban development--Asia. | Urbanization--Asia. | Urban renewal--Asia.
Classification: LCC HT243.A77 C43 2016 | DDC 307.3/416095--dc23
LC record available at https://lccn.loc.gov/2016008380

British Library Cataloguing-in-Publication Data
A catalogue record for this book is available from the British Library.

Desk Editor: Dong Lixi

Typeset by Stallion Press
Email: enquiries@stallionpress.com

Contents

About the Editors and Contributors

John WONG is Professorial Fellow and academic adviser at the East Asian Institute (EAI), National University of Singapore. Previously, he was Research Director at EAI and Director of the Institute of East Asian Political Economy. Professor Wong also taught at the University of Hong Kong, the National University of Singapore and Florida State University. He had held visiting appointments at Harvard University's Fairbank Centre, Yale's Economic Growth Centre, Oxford University's St Antony's College and Stanford University's economics department. He also held the ASEAN chair at the University of Toronto. Professor Wong has written and edited 35 books and published more than 500 articles and papers on China and other East Asian economies. He has also circulated over 90 policy-related reports to the Singapore government. He holds a PhD in economics from the University of London.

LYE Liang Fook is Assistant Director and Research Fellow at the EAI, National University of Singapore. His research interests cover China's central-local relations, political legitimacy, the print media, China-ASEAN relations and China-Singapore relations. He was part of a team that completed a study on the Suzhou Industrial Park, a flagship project between China and Singapore. He has also conducted research on the Sino-Singapore Tianjin Eco-city project, the second flagship project between China and Singapore. He attended the Hanban programme for distinguished scholars in China studies in 2009. His publications have appeared in Routledge, *International Relations of the Asia Pacific, Journal of Chinese Political Science*, Eastern Universities Press, Institute of Southeast Asian Studies (ISEAS) Publishing, Konrad Adenauer Stiftung Publishing, World Scientific Press and *China: An International Journal*. Besides his involvement in the academia, he manages the Singapore Secretariat of the Network of East Asian Think Tanks (NEAT) and the Network of ASEAN-China Think Tanks (NACT), two Track II bodies that aim to foster ASEAN Plus Three cooperation and ASEAN Plus One cooperation, respectively.

KHOO Teng Chye is Executive Director of the Centre for Liveable Cities. He was previously Chief Executive of PUB, Singapore's national water agency, Chief Executive Officer/Chief Planner of Urban Redevelopment Authority, Chief Executive Officer/Group President of PSA Corporation, President and Chief Executive Officer of Mapletree Investments and Managing Director (Special Projects) of Temasek Holdings. He sits on the boards of Tropical Marine Science Institute of National University of Singapore (NUS) and GDF Suez's Urban Strategy Council. He is a member of the Advisory Board of World Future Foundation, the Advisory Committee for the School of Civil and Environmental Engineering at Nanyang Technological University (NTU), the Advisory Panel of NUSDeltares and the Advisory Group of Singapore Management University's Master of Tri-Sector Collaboration Programme. He is also an adjunct professor at NTU's School of Civil and Environmental Engineering (CEE) and Lee Kuan Yew School of Public Policy at NUS. He is a member of the Jurong Lake District Steering Committee, as well as the Advisory Committee for the formation of the new capital for the state of Andhra Pradesh, India. He graduated with First Class Honours in Civil Engineering from Monash University, Australia. A President-cum-Colombo Plan scholar, he also holds a Master of Science in Construction Engineering and a Master of Business Administration from NUS. He is a fellow of the Institution of Engineers, Singapore and attended the Advanced Management Programme at Harvard Business School. He was awarded the Public

Administration (Gold) in 1996 and the Public Administration (Silver) in 1987 by the Singapore government. He was also conferred the Meritorious Service Award by the National Trade Union Congress in 2008 for his contributions to the Singapore Labour Movement.

ZHAO Litao is Senior Research Fellow at the EAI, National University of Singapore. He obtained his PhD in sociology from Stanford University. His research interests include social stratification and mobility, sociology of education, organisational analysis and China's social policy. His research has appeared in *China Quarterly, Research in Social Stratification and Mobility, International Journal of Educational Development, Social Sciences in China, Built Environment, China: An International Journal, East Asian Policy, Frontiers of Education in China, Issues and Studies,* and so on. He has authored, co-authored, edited or co-edited six books, including *China's Social Development and Policy* (Routledge 2013) and *Singapore's Social Development in Transition* (in Chinese, World Scientific 2013).

PHAM Thuy Loan is Deputy Director of the Vietnam National Institute of Architecture (VIAr) in the Ministry of Construction, Vietnam. She began her career in urban planning and design since 2004 upon completion of her master's and doctorate programme in Urban Design Laboratory at the Department of Urban Engineering in the University of Tokyo. She then worked in the Department of Urban Planning at the National University of Civil Engineering (NUCE) from 2004 to 2014. She became the head of the department since 2008 until she moved to the VIAr in the Ministry of Construction. She was involved in a wide spectrum of urban design and planning projects such as The Study for Roadside Station Master Plan in the Socialist Republic of Vietnam (2007–2008), Socio-economic Development Strategy for Long An Province until 2020 and the Vision for 2030 (2009–2010), Provincial Development Strategy for Quang Nam Province (2010–2011), The Study on the Comprehensive Urban Development Programme in Hanoi Capital City (2004–2005), Integrated Urban Development for Urban Mass Rapid Transportation Development for Hanoi (2009), Master

Plan for Da Nang City and the Surrounding Region (2008–2010) and other projects of smaller scales. Her current interests focus on improving the legal framework of urban planning and design in Vietnam, as well as technical practices in the field of planning and design.

Adoracion M NAVARRO is Senior Research Fellow at the Philippine Institute for Development Studies (PIDS). Her research interests cover energy, transport and water supply infrastructure. She writes and contributes her insights to the macroeconomic analysis and growth outlook sections of the PIDS flagship publication called *Economic Policy Monitor*. She also contributes to the body of knowledge on ASEAN matters through various research under the auspices of regional institutions such as the Economic Research Institute for ASEAN and East Asia in Jakarta and the ASEAN Studies Center in Bangkok. She holds a PhD in economics from the University of the Philippines-Diliman and an MPA in economic policy management from Columbia University-New York.

Mazlena MAZLAN is a columnist at Malaysia's *New Straits Times*, focusing on a wide range of socio-economic and development issues such as human capital development, labour market, technical and vocational education and training, women in economic development and Malaysia's economic issues in general. She was a researcher with the Institute of Strategic and International Studies (ISIS) Malaysia in the Economics Unit until September 2014 before joining a top government-linked company in Kuala Lumpur. She is also an independent economic analyst with her views being featured in the Malaysian print and electronic media. She was the project manager and editor for *Housing the Nation: Policies, Issues and Prospects* published by Cagamas Holdings Berhad in 2013. Mazlena received her bachelor's and master's degrees from the London School of Economics and Political Science, United Kingdom.

ZHOU Zhihua is a Visiting Research Fellow at the East Asian Institute, National University of Singapore. She worked in top property companies in China for several years before pursuing her further studies in the United Kingdom. She obtained her master's in development economics from the Department of Economics and PhD in urban studies at the Department of Urban Studies and Planning at Sheffield University. Her research mainly focuses on the built environment in the East Asian context, including land use management and urbanisation, housing tenure and real estate economics, urban regeneration and heritage conservation, sustainable construction and environmental governance.

CUI Haining is Associate Professor and Research Fellow at the Institute of Asian Studies, China Foreign Affairs University. She holds a PhD in international politics from Renmin University of China. Her current research interests cover East Asian regionalism, food security and poverty reduction cooperation. Her main publications include *The Balance between Interests and Values: The Study on Adjustment and Theoretical Orientation of Post-Cold War U.S. National Security Strategy* (Economic Science Publishing House 2014), *The Predicament of East Asian Food Security Cooperation and China's Role* (Foreign Affairs Review 2014) and "ASEAN Plus Three Cooperation", *East Asia Cooperation 2012* (Economic Science Publishing House 2013). She has been involved in joint research and other relevant works of the Network of East Asian Think Tanks (NEAT) and the Network of ASEAN-China Think Tanks (NACT) since the two Track II mechanisms were established.

KIM Joo-Young is a PhD candidate at Department of Archaeology and Cultural Anthropology in Chonbuk National University of Korea. Her anthropological research interests cover Korea's urban poverty areas, life of the poor, poverty tourism and inequality issues. She completed a study on Public Parks as a socio-cultural space for the marginal people in 2014. Now, she is a part of the project team to help the poor community lead an active and vibrant lifestyle via cultural activities. For her doctoral dissertation, she is conducting a field work at impoverished areas in small-sized cities of Korea, examining the current development projects in those areas.

Kaoru ISHIKAWA is trustee of Kawamura Gakuen, an incorporated educational institution and Specially Appointed Professor at Kawamura Gakuen Women's University. He also teaches at Akita International University as Visiting Professor, and the University of Tokyo (Graduate School of Arts and Science), Waseda University (Graduate School of Asia-Pacific studies) and Meiji University as part-time lecturer. As former senior diplomat (Director General of Multilateral Cooperation Department, Director General of Economic Affairs Bureau, Ambassador to Egypt, to Arab League and then to Canada), he has been in charge of humanitarian assistance, poverty eradication, promotion of human security, global rule-making of trade and investment and G7 (G8) summit preparations, among others. He continues to be interested in those issues and teaches human security, political science, African politics and international relations. He has published extensively on development and global governance, including *Nation Building and Development Assistance in Africa* (Macmillan Press Ltd 1999) and *African Fire* (in Japanese, Gakuseisha 1992). He is the author and editor of 'Togoh EC no subete' (EC's integration) (in Japanese, Nihon Keizai Shimbun 1992) and co-author of several books including *External Factors for Asian Development* (Institute of Southeast Asian Studies 2003) and *Ryutaro Hashimoto* (in Japanese, Bungei-shunju Ltd 2012). Besides the academia, he is the Managing Director of Japan-Canada Association that promotes friendship between the two people and Director of the Society for Promotion of Japanese Diplomacy that enhances international mutual understanding.

Introduction

Urbanisation and Development: An Overview

John WONG and LYE Liang Fook*

A new wave of urbanisation

Urbanisation has always been an important part of economic and social development. Over the past few decades, the world has witnessed a wave of urban explosion. In 1900, only 13% of the world's population (about 220 million) lived in towns and cities.[1] In 1950, the proportion increased to 29% with urban population more than trebling to 746 million. By 2005, the proportion further increased to 49% with the total urban population hitting 3.2 billion. By mid-2007, the world's total urban population exceeded that of rural population.[2]

*John Wong is Professorial Fellow of the East Asian Institute at the National University of Singapore. Lye Liang Fook is Assistant Director and Research Fellow at the same institute.

[1] Cities have been around since the third millennium BC. And as long as they have existed, people have been drawn to them for what they offer. As recently as 1800, however, only 2% of the world's population lived in urban areas. See United Nations Center for Human Settlement (Habitat), "Istanbul + 5: The United Nations Special Session of the General Assembly for an Overall Review and Appraisal of the Implementation of the Habitat Agenda, New York, 6-8 June 2001", at <http://www.un.org/ga/Istanbul+5/brochure.pdf> (accessed 15 July 2014).

[2] United Nations, "Population of Urban and Rural Areas at Mid-Year (thousands) and Percentage Urban, 2014", *World Urbanization Prospects* (the 2014 revision),

This has given rise to the new "urban millennium" — one of the most critical global trends that governments will have to grapple with.

A few interesting observations about the urbanisation process over the years and in the future are worth highlighting here. First, most of the urban growth over the past few decades came from the developing world, partly because the developed countries have attained a relatively high rate of urbanisation. In 1950 only about 17% of the population in developing countries lived in towns and cities. In 1985, about 32% of the populations in developing countries were urbanised, compared to around 71% in the developed world. By 2010, the proportion of urban population in the developing world reached 46%, compared to 77% in the developed world.[3]

Second, the rate of urbanisation in the developing world, particularly developing countries in Africa and Asia, is expected to accelerate much more. In 2014, it was observed that high levels of urbanisation, at 80% and above, are already prevalent in Latin America and the Caribbean, and North America. By 2050, urbanisation level is expected to hit above 85%. In Europe today, 73% of the population live in urban areas and this is expected to rise to over 80% by 2050.

By contrast, Africa and Asia remain largely rural, with urban populations accounting for 40% and 48%, respectively, in 2014. By 2050, Africa and Asia is expected to urbanise at a much faster rate than other regions, attaining an urbanisation rate of 56% and 64%, respectively.[4]

Population Division, Department of Economic and Social Affairs, United Nations, at <http://esa.un.org/unpd/wup/CD-ROM/Default.aspx> (accessed 15 July 2014).

[3] United Nations, "Percentage of Population at Mid-Year Residing in Urban Areas by Major Area, Region and Country, 1950–2050", *World Urbanization Prospects* (the 2014 revision), Population Division, Department of Economic and Social Affairs, United Nations, at <http://esa.un.org/unpd/wup/CD-ROM/Default.aspx> (accessed 15 July 2014).

[4] United Nations, "*World Urbanization Prospects* (the 2014 revision)", Population Division, Department of Economic and Social Affairs, United Nations, p. 7, at <http://esa.un.org/unpd/wup/Highlights/WUP2014-Highlights.pdf> (accessed 15 July 2014).

Third, Africa and Asia are also expected to "blaze a trail" in terms of their overall contribution to the size of the urban population in the years ahead. It is forecast that by 2050, nearly 2.5 billion people will be added to the world's urban population which currently stands at 3.9 billion. Close to 90% of the 2.5 billion increase in the world's urban population is expected to take place in the urban areas of Africa and Asia. By 2050, it has been projected that most of the urban population of the world will be concentrated in Asia (52%) and Africa (21%).

Three countries from Asia and Africa, namely China, India and Nigeria, are projected to account for 37% of the increase of nearly 2.5 billion people in the urban population by 2050. In particular, between 2014 and 2050, the population in urban areas is expected to grow by 404 million people in India, 292 million in China and 212 million in Nigeria. The projected urban population increase in other Asian countries such as Indonesia, Bangladesh and Pakistan is more than 50 million each.[5]

In sum, the urbanisation rate in Africa and Asia is expected to accelerate in the years ahead, and both regions are envisaged to contribute to a large proportion of the increase in the world's urban population. Furthermore, future increases in the world's population are expected to be highly concentrated in a few countries largely confined to Africa and Asia.

The causes of urbanisation

What is the definition of urbanisation? In simple terms, urbanisation refers to the "growth of towns and cities", and the process is marked by the movement of population from rural areas to urban areas. Urbanisation is basically spurred by industrialisation progress, with people leaving agricultural and farming occupations in rural areas for manufacturing and service jobs in towns and cities.

In recent years, the urbanisation process has been further catalysed by globalisation, causing intense competition among cities. Cities, in

[5] United Nations, "*World Urbanization Prospects* (the 2014 revision)", pp. 11–12.

different countries and even within a country, now engage in intense competition with one another to attract talent and capital. To do so, many city-governing authorities offer attractive financial incentives in addition to providing practical conveniences such as well-functioning infrastructure, urban services and communication systems, efficient transport, adequate housing and access to educational and recreational facilities. Such modern-day conveniences and attractive incentives have made cities even more appealing not only for people to move out of rural areas but also to migrate between cities.

Urban growth, in a fundamental sense, stems from three basic sources: (i) natural internal population growth in the cities; (ii) in-migration from the rural areas; and (iii) administrative changes.[6] To begin with, urban total fertility rates (TFR) everywhere are bound to decline over time, especially in comparison with those in rural areas. Demographers recognise that urban living and the overall urban environment are economically and socially not conducive to the formation of large family size for the following factors: housing pressures, the nuclear family structure, high costs of bringing up children in an urban setting, the opportunity cost of getting married earlier and having more children for women, and the opportunity cost of having more leisure activities for parents are all "anti-natal" in nature, i.e. forces that work against families with too many children. Hence rapid and continuing fertility decline is a worldwide trend in almost all cities.

This brings to the fore rural-urban migration as the single most important source of urban growth. Most cities are inundated with the constant influx of rural migrants. There are many economic and social reasons for the exodus of rural people bound for the cities. In most developing countries, their rural areas are overpopulated and the income earned from selling agriculture products is low. This in turn gives rise to rural poverty and serious rural unemployment or underemployment (i.e. zero marginal productivity for the extra agricultural worker).

---

[6] For further discussion on relevant issues of urbanisation, see John D. Kasarda and Edward M. Crenshaw, "Third World Urbanization: Dimensions, Theories, and Determinants", *Annual Review of Sociology*, vol. 17, August 1991, pp. 467–501.

Peasants therefore flock to cities to seek better economic opportunities. This is the basic "push" factor for migration.

Located mainly around the cities, manufacturing industries offer many employment opportunities to rural migrants. In the cities, myriads of service jobs from construction and building to various openings in the "informal sector" (comprising low-paying service activities like street peddling and hawking) attract rural migrants. Thus, the Todaro model of migration postulates that migration decision depends on the expected income differentials between rural and urban areas as well as the probability of getting employment.[7] Better job prospects and the more widely available social and recreational amenities in the urban areas provide rural migrants access to a better quality of life than if they were to remain in the countryside. All of these constitute the "pull factors" of urban living.

Finally, the "growth" of cities can also be changed by pure administrative measures, i.e. by redefining or redrawing the city limits or boundaries or by re-designating the employment status of the population. A good example of such practice is China. What constitutes an urban or rural population — i.e. whether a person's *hukou* (household registration) is in the cities or the countryside — has, until in recent years, been largely an administrative matter. Such administrative intervention has artificially hampered the natural process of rural-urban migration, severely limiting the growth of cities in China. On the other hand, China's administrative decisions to designate a city (e.g. Chongqing) by including many surrounding rural counties and townships have also exaggerated the rate of urban growth.

The economic rationale for urban growth

Since rural migration is the major source of urban growth, this gives rise to the question: How can the rural sector continue to release its agricultural labour for the cities? According to W. Arthur Lewis's

---

[7] See Michael P. Todaro and Stephen C Smith, *Economic Development*, Boston, Pearson Addison Wesley, 2009.

two-sector theory of economic growth, the agricultural or traditional sector has unlimited supply of labour that will eventually be transferred to the urban areas (the modern sector) for industrial development. The process will go on until the rural labour supply curve has reached a turning point whereby marginal product of rural labour is positive, i.e. there is no more surplus labour.[8]

Gustav Ranis and John Fei refined Lewis' theory and elaborated the process of transferring agricultural surplus to urban areas, based on the East Asian development experiences. The first step is to raise agricultural productivity per unit of labour so as to produce a transferable "total agricultural surplus", i.e. "labor plus food" for industrial development in urban areas.[9] This means that a strong agricultural foundation is the basis for successful industrialisation (or urbanisation). In other words, an agricultural take-off has to precede the industrial take-off.

In the least developed economies, about 70% to 80% of their labour force is peasants living at subsistence level. In pre-industrial Japan and Taiwan, over 80% of their labour force was also peasants or farmers. Today, farmers in Japan and Taiwan — many of them being part-time farmers as the bulk of their incomes are derived from non-farm earnings — constitute less than 5% of labour force in the country. In other words, both Japan and Taiwan had achieved an agricultural revolution before their industrial revolution and urbanisation. Rising agricultural productivity makes it possible for more rural labour to be released for non-farm activities away from the rural areas. In this regard, the roots of successful urbanisation can essentially be traced back to successful agricultural development.

Granted that industrialisation is the underlying cause of urbanisation, the next question is: How can cities continue to grow so rapidly? Urban growth, like economic growth, ultimately depends on productivity growth. What are the sources of urban productivity growth?

---

[8] W. Arthur Lewis, "Economic Development with Unlimited Supplies of Labour", *The Manchester School*, vol. 22, no. 2, May 1954, pp. 139–191.

[9] G. Ranis and J.C.H. Fei, *Development of the Labour Surplus Economy: Theory and Policy*, New York, Richard D. Irwin Inc., 1964.

Cities are clusters of peoples and activities. The basic economic rationale behind the growth of cities is the concentration of people and production. The concentration of productive resources in cities has produced many positive "agglomeration effects" comprising both "economies of scale" and "external economies". Productivity rises as the scale of production increases. Industries can also reap extra benefits if they are located in close proximity and are complementary to each other, i.e. the Marshall's external economies.[10]

External economies can also occur when many small cities or suburbs establish their economic linkages with each other to produce the regional integration effect. Such urban integration gives rise to the concept of megacities (with more than 10 million inhabitants) or large cities (of between five to 10 million inhabitants).[11] A larger-scale urban integration is the Pearl River Delta. Furthermore, any big city can be externally integrated, e.g. Hong Kong, Singapore and even Shanghai are all linking up to the world. In short, both internal and external integration can generate productivity (or extra benefits) needed for rapid urban growth.

While there are benefits to urbanisation, there are downsides as well. One of which is the problem of negative externalities as production facilities are over-concentrated. Pollution worsens when industries are clustered too close to each other. Increasing population density in cities causes congestion and social discomfort or even social discontent due

---

[10] World Bank, "Scale Economies and Agglomeration", *World Development Report 2009*, chapter 4.

[11] In 1990, there were 10 megacities with more than 10 million inhabitants, representing less than 7% of the global urban population. In 2014, the number of megacities nearly tripled to 28 with a total population of 453 million, accounting for 12% of the world's urban dwellers. Tokyo is the world's largest city with a total of 38 million inhabitants, followed by Delhi with 25 million, Shanghai with 23 million, and Mexico City, Mumbai and Sao Paulo, each with around 21 million inhabitants. See United Nations, "*World Urbanization Prospects* (the 2014 revision)", p. 13, Population Division, Department of Economic and Social Affairs, United Nations, at <http://esa.un.org/unpd/wup/Highlights/WUP2014-Highlights.pdf> (accessed 15 July 2014).

to overcrowding. Other challenges include the emergence of slums and illegal settlers, high energy consumption and large waste generation. Apart from these challenges, it is important to recognise that not all cities are as well-equipped or ready to handle the existing urban population explosion or future influx of urban migrants.

However, the future is not all gloom and doom. For one, continuing technical innovations and technological progress (e.g. high-rise living that takes into account certain environmentally-friendly features) and more investment in social amenities can help to alleviate these negative externalities.

Furthermore, unlike the old concepts of agglomeration economies which are primarily based on the beneficial effects arising from the concentration of industries and physical capital in the cities, new economic growth theory, focusing on human capital formation leveraging on technology, promises greater potential of urban growth that is based on the formation of cluster of human capital. It is clear that cities are usually centres of education and research, which naturally promotes human resource development.[12]

According to Robert Lucas, even migrant labour can acquire skills required by modern production technologies through on-the-job training. He optimistically foresees the eventual transformation of a 90% agricultural economy to a 90% urban economy for most countries because of the human capital formation potential. With continuing technological progress and human capital accumulation, cities of the future are envisaged to become liveable "intelligent cities" with a knowledge-based economy.

The critical role of governments in urbanisation

As urbanisation in Asia is expected to accelerate and gain greater dominance in terms of proportion of the world's urban population, it is important to ensure that the urbanisation process is properly managed.

[12] Robert E. Lucas, "Life Earnings and Rural-Urban Migration", *Journal of Political Economy*, vol. 112, no. S1, 2004, pp. S29–S59.

Here, governments, whether at the national or city levels, and other stakeholders can play a critical role in ensuring positive outcomes for urban residents.

The state largely performs three basic functions in the urbanisation process. First, the state's primary function is to maintain basic law and order, and provide public amenities and services such as public sanitation and waste disposal. Second, the state performs a regulatory role in setting up and revising the "rules of the game" for urban growth. Third, the state is involved in and participates in the urbanisation process. Over the years, there has been a rethink of the state's role in the overall economic and social development process. The ideas about what the state can do or should do for urbanisation have also been changing.

It is commonly agreed that in the early phases of urbanisation, when the mainstay of the economy is still primarily rural or agricultural, the government's role should be as neutral as possible. At this stage, the state should focus its role in establishing the basic institutional framework to facilitate urban growth. It could begin with implementing a sound land policy and provide some essential services and basic infrastructure. The growth and development of a city should be based on its own geographical and economic comparative advantage. At the incipient phase of urbanisation, it is often difficult for the city government to forecast accurately how the city will develop in future, particularly since it cannot control or influence the political and economic dynamics of development in its rural hinterlands or adjacent regions.

In places that experience rapid urbanisation, as in most Chinese cities today, the government's role is deemed to be more crucial because active intervention is often required. Rapid urbanisation is the stage that requires the government's extensive involvement in many large-scale infrastructure projects, from mass transit to port and airport development. In addition, the state is responsible for the revision and implementation of the city's master plan, and other new social infrastructure involving education, health care and recreation. It also has to deal with problems of population density and overcrowding, and formulate various policies and measures to control pollution and promote environment protection. And all of these activities cost money. Thus, a good and effective government is one that accords sufficient priority to economic growth by taking appropriate measures to attract investment and promote business expansion. In short, the most important economic agenda for a modern city is to create employment, and the most important social and environmental agenda is to make the city liveable.

For many mature cities at advanced stage of urbanisation, the government is faced with a different set of problems. The government's immediate task could range from refurbishing or rebuilding the city's old economic and social infrastructure to drafting policies for slum clearance and urban renewal. It is however a greater imperative for the government to restructure or reinvigorate the city's economy. This may involve a reorientation of its traditional economy in light of the shifting comparative advantage of the city. When the economy of the city's hinterlands or its adjacent regions has changed, the city has to adapt to and find new sources for its economic growth.

In the final analysis, what a state can do or how much it can do depends on whether the government has the requisite financial resources. This is the public finance angle of urbanisation, which is an important component in ensuring that whatever plans or measures related to urbanisation can be implemented. Suffice it to say that the government's active participation in urbanisation is, financially speaking, often very expensive. As people live in close proximity to each other in urban areas, there is a need for a wide range of public services and basic infrastructure, which are costly to build and maintain. These are, however, the basic costs for maintaining the city. If the city aspires to upgrade itself to an environmentally friendly, culturally vibrant and socially liveable city, it needs even more costly investments. Thus, it all boils down to the key public finance questions of whether the city has a viable revenue base or if it has some feasible long-term financing mechanisms.

This then brings to the fore the central issue of what the state should be doing or what it can best do in the area of urbanisation. Should the state be involved in all of those activities mentioned earlier? Can some of these functions be left to the market, the private sector or non-governmental organisations? There is no economics textbook to tell us how much the government should be involved in economic or urban development. There is no such thing as the "optimal" extent of government involvement in economic and social development, much depending on the history, the political culture, the institutional structure of a particular government, and even on the timing. In other words, this debate on the extent of government involvement is largely an ideological issue.

In the immediate post-war period, the government was considered a prime mover for initiating economic development, particularly for developing countries that lacked an effectively functioning market and entrepreneurship. Market failure led to more government intervention. But the 1980s saw a sharp turnaround, with both academic and political circles reacting against extensive government intervention. Government was seen as a "problem", particularly in the United States under the Reagan administration and in the United Kingdom under Margaret Thatcher. As a result, more focus was put on "government failure" and how misguided government intervention had led to price distortion, inefficiencies, wastefulness and misallocation of resources. The resulting orthodoxy was "small government" and "more market". The central doctrine then was "getting the price right".[13]

In the post-financial crisis world with the "Washington Consensus" losing much of its lustre (especially in the wake of the 2008 financial crisis), the proper role of the government in economic and social development, and hence also in urbanisation, is being re-assessed again. In future, the right approach to this issue may require a more open-minded and less ideological stance. The government is more likely to take a more balanced and mixed role.

In the area of urban development, a lot of essential public services like safety and security, and environmental protection are public goods that should be left to the government to take care. Other basic infrastructure such as public utilities like water supply and electricity are also public goods, but their provision and management can best be left

---

[13] For further discussion on the changing role of the state in economic development, see World Bank, *World Development Report 1997*.

to the market for greater efficiency and better conservation. Many activities can also be organised under some kind of public-private partnership. Particularly for the developing countries, it is simply very hard to generalise what should be best handled by the government and what should be best done by the market.

Rather than be mired in an unproductive ideological debate on the extent of government involvement in urbanisation, a better approach is to highlight certain operating principles or practices that can serve as a reference for governments. The following could include the involvement of governments:

(i) ensuring that cities maintain their economic growth and vibrancy so as to generate the necessary employment opportunities and, at the same time, provide a viable revenue base;
(ii) creating an environment conducive to the growth of cities (including playing a positive regulatory role that encompasses an integrated and cross-sectoral approach);
(iii) providing leadership in certain aspects of the urbanisation process when required (such as formulating and reviewing the "rules of the game" for urbanisation) and refraining from getting involved when better options or alternatives exist;
(iv) adopting an open and inclusive approach through working with various stakeholders (such as the private sector, civil society, non-governmental organisations and external partners) to leverage on their strengths.

Last but not least, it is extremely useful for countries to share their experiences on urbanisation with one another so that they can benefit from best practices and avoid the mistakes made. In this connection, this collection of articles brings together the perspectives of selected countries of the ASEAN Plus Three such as Singapore, Vietnam, the Philippines, Malaysia, China, Korea and Japan. Each of the anthors elaborates on the process of urbanisation in his or her respective countries and highlights the achievements and challenges encountered.

Although all of these countries are at different stages of development and face different circumstances, they are all confronted with the common challenge of managing the process of urbanisation (whether urban expansion, urban renewal or a combination of both) so as to improve the quality of life for residents in urban areas and to make cities liveable.

While the focus is on bringing quality lifestyle to people in an urban setting, it is also important to recognise that the development of the rural areas should proceed hand in hand. After all, rural and urban areas are but both sides of the same coin and ought to be taken as a whole if the process of urbanisation is to be a comprehensive and integrated one.

Chapter 1

Building a Liveable City: The Singapore Experience

KHOO Teng Chye*

Introduction

With over 5.5 million inhabitants living on 720 square kilometres of land, Singapore today is one of only a few cities in the world recognised for achieving high standards of liveability and sustainable development, despite a high population density. This would have been difficult to imagine in the 1960s when Singapore was plagued by economic woes, poor infrastructure and squalid conditions and populated by about 1.7 million people, a third of the present population. This leap, from a developing nation to a thriving global metropolis ranked among the world's most liveable cities in the space of 40 years, was the result of decades of deliberate planning and implementation that sought to strike a balance between density, development and liveability.

In 2008, the Centre for Liveable Cities (CLC) was established to capture the explicit and tacit knowledge underlying Singapore's unique

* KHOO Teng Chye is Executive Director of the Centre for Liveable Cities, Singapore.

urban development experience, and to distil some of the general principles that have guided Singapore's urban planners and policy makers over the years. Its research has covered over 130 original interviews with past and present cabinet ministers and senior officials, several of whom are quoted in this chapter. Through its research, CLC found that Singapore has held three key outcomes constant in its pursuit of liveable urban development:

(i) A **competitive economy** in order to attract investments and provide jobs;
(ii) A **sustainable environment** because the city has to survive with limited natural resources, especially in terms of land and water; and
(iii) A **high quality of life**, including the social and psychological well-being of the population.

In addition to these three outcomes, two elements have been vital to successful urbanisation in Singapore. First, it was crucial to have a system of integrated planning and development that kept the outcomes of a liveable city constantly in view, over the long term.

Second, subscribing to an urban governance approach that was dynamic helped sustain the conditions needed for a thriving liveable city.

Together, these elements form the components of the CLC Liveability Framework (Figure 1).[1]

The liveable city outcomes

In 1992, the United Nations Conference on Environment and Development (UNCED) posited that the social, environmental and economic needs of a country must be met but in balance with one another. There are however no absolute levels whereby liveability is met. Instead, the challenge is to optimise the trade-offs at each stage of

[1] Khoo Teng Chye, et al (eds), *Liveable and Sustainable Cities: a Framework*, Singapore, Centre for Liveable Cities and Civil Service College, 2014.

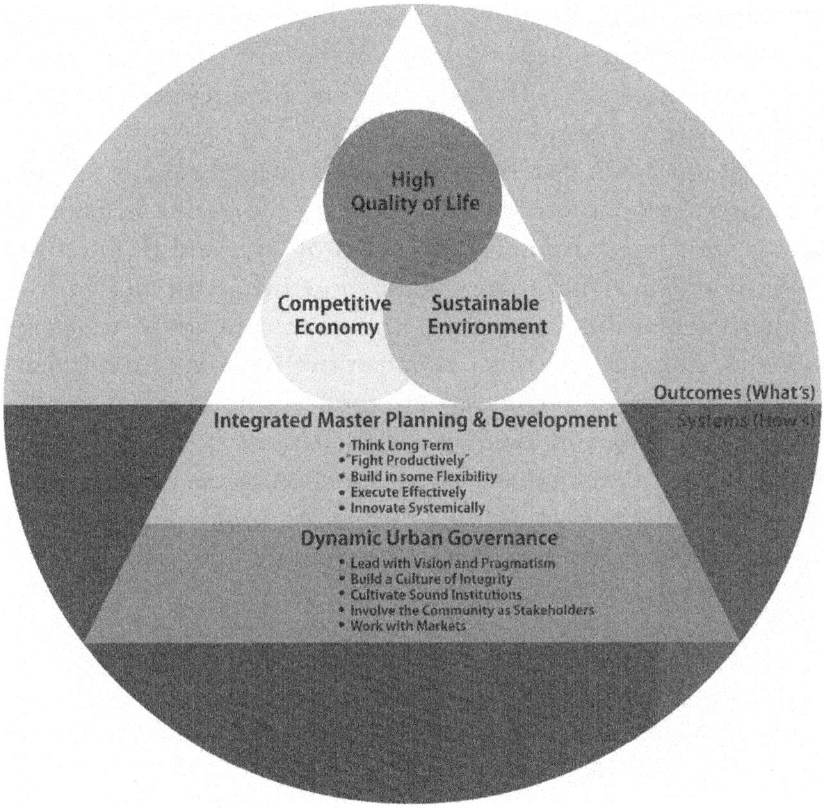

Figure 1. CLC Liveability Framework

Source: Centre for Liveable Cities.

growth. Hence, each city must take into account its own needs, resources and context when planning its development.

The philosophy behind the liveable city outcomes identified in the CLC Framework has nevertheless remained consistent for more than four decades of Singapore's development.

Outcome 1: A competitive economy

Singapore's competitive economy has contributed greatly to the city-state's liveability quotient. At the most basic level, residents need opportunities to make a living and achieve a degree of economic security. This is as true today as it was in the early days of development when industrialisation helped squatters and rural residents transit to a modern urban economy.

Singapore's urban systems have had an integral role in supporting the country's economic development — a priority in its earliest years — from the purposeful allocation of land and facilities to the supply of utilities and a strong transport infrastructure with local and global connections, giving the economy a competitive edge over its regional neighbours.[2] In turn, a competitive economy has allowed the city-state to generate income to sustain itself, develop and create yet more opportunities for growth in a virtuous cycle.

With further development, a well-functioning economy and a liveable environment have become ever more important, since cities worldwide now compete for investment and mobile talent:

> *If the people are rooted to the place, that's how you can help ensure that there's a certain robustness to it and even for those who are foreigners ... the liveability and vibrancy are important ... To the extent that we can root them through clustering of knowledge and people and like-minded activities, we will do that.*[3]
>
> *Beh Swan Gin, former managing director, Economic Development Board*

Outcome 2: A sustainable environment

Singapore was committed to sustainable development early on in order to preserve and make the most of what few natural resources it had. Provisions for clean air, clean water and green cover were integral to city

---

[2] Lee Kuan Yew, interview by the Centre for Liveable Cities, Singapore, 31 August 2012. Lee was Singapore's first prime minister, from 1959 to 1990. An edited version of the interview transcript was published in *Urban Solutions* no. 2, February 2013.

[3] Beh Swan Gin, interview by the Centre for Liveable Cities, Singapore, 21 February 2012. Beh is currently permanent secretary of the Ministry of Law. He was managing director of the Economic Development Board, among other appointments.

planning from the start. Careful thought was even given to wind patterns for the location of industrial estates to the west of Singapore to prevent the spread of air pollution to the city. When Japanese company Sumitomo wanted to build a petrochemical plant in the mid-1970s, pollution control requirements threatened to raise costs and deter the project:

> *But the Ministry of Environment said, "No, we should not concede. It will pollute Singapore." This went to Cabinet and Cabinet agreed with the Ministry of Environment. They said, "No, we insist." Then Sumitomo proceeded and put in the investments necessary.*[4]
>
> *S Dhanabalan, former Cabinet minister*

Environmental considerations have not been assumed to be at odds with economic development. Instead, they have been integrated into urban planning and embedded into a larger social and economic narrative by framing them as a means to distinguish Singapore from its regional peers. In the early years, a clean and green city was a way to show foreign investors that Singapore was a well-run country and thus a good and pleasant place to set up business.

Outcome 3: A high quality of life

The notion of a high quality of life encompasses many aspects of urban living, including economic, social, environmental and psychological. A key part of Singapore's attraction today is its pleasant and well-planned environment — a far cry from the early days of slums, squalor and crime. Indeed, apart from the provision of amenities, creating a sense of personal security was an important aspect of developing

---

[4] S Dhanabalan, interview by the Centre for Liveable Cities, Singapore, 20 December 2011. Dhanabalan was former chairman of Temasek Holdings (Pte) Ltd. He held previous appointments as minister for Foreign Affairs, minister for Culture, minister for Community Development, minister for National Development, and minister for Trade and Industry.

Singapore's new towns:

> *Create a sense of safety ... It is no use having good surroundings, if you are afraid all the time ... We have Neighbourhood Police Posts — police who know the people in that neighbourhood, so they know when strangers come in.*[5]
>
> *Lee Kuan Yew, former prime minister*

Retaining a sense of engagement in the physical landscape has since become a way to encourage Singaporeans to feel connected to the land. Since the mid-1980s, city planning in Singapore has also tried to give more emphasis to the character and soul of the city-state, one that encompasses culture, identity and aesthetics.

Balancing the three liveability outcomes

These three liveable city outcomes are linked directly to Singapore's outcome indicators at the national level. They are published in the Ministry of Finance's Revenue and Expenditure Estimates for each financial year, ensuring that all government agencies know the big picture of the overall state of urban development. It also signals to the public that the government is committed to and serious about making Singapore liveable.

Developing a liveable Singapore involves balancing the three interdependent (and often overlapping) outcomes. Focusing too much on one at the expense of the others could easily lead to undesirable outcomes. Nor are the outcomes always so discrete: solutions to achieve one outcome could create opportunities towards another.

For instance, Singapore's quest for water self-sufficiency has given rise to a niche sector of specialised companies that provide water reclamation and desalination services. With further investment by the government, this nascent water sector is now expected to provide 11,000 jobs and add S$1.7 billion to the economy by 2015.

Taken together, these three outcomes form Singapore's planning and development regime.

---

[5] Lee Kuan Yew, interview by the Centre for Liveable Cities, Singapore, 31 August 2012.

Integrated master planning: implicit principles

Singapore's integrated master planning system has enabled the government to create and manage urban systems that balance the different guiding priorities on both short- and long-term scales in response to changes in a dynamic political, economic and social environment. A key differentiating factor for Singapore's planning regime is that its plans do not just stay on paper — they are implemented and executed through dedicated organisations, with expertise and resources. Five implicit principles underpin Singapore's integrated master planning approach.

Principle 1: Think long term

At the heart of the integrated master planning approach is Singapore's overarching Concept Plan, covering the country's land use over a time horizon of up to 50 years. The plan, created through an inter-agency effort, ensures that all key land use requirements for the city are met and that individual urban systems, such as transport, water or public housing, do not work in isolation.

Taking a long-term view has been important in two other ways. First, it has helped officials keep the three liveability outcomes in balance, at both the planning and implementing stages. Second, taking a long-term view has helped the government identify problems in the future, making it expedient to take steps to pre-empt the problem or to develop a good project ahead of its time. In the early decades of Singapore's rapid growth, even longer planning time frames were needed:

> *[We made] a decision to project to 'Year X' which was 100 years. Why? Because I said to myself that if we don't do that, we will certainly run out of land. [We may] build to too low a density when you project for the short term. And then we run out of space.*[6]
>
> *Liu Thai Ker, former CEO, Housing and Development Board and Urban Redevelopment Authority and chairman, Centre for Liveable Cities*

[6] Liu Thai Ker, interview by the Centre for Liveable Cities, Singapore, 16 September 2011. Liu is currently director of RSP Architects Planners & Engineers (Pte) Ltd. He held previous appointments as chief executive officer of the Housing and Development Board and Urban Redevelopment Authority.

Principle 2: Fight productively

Left to its own devices, each government agency would focus on its own targets rather than the goals of the government as a whole. In order to facilitate integrated planning, an inter-agency structure is needed to encourage agencies to acknowledge one another's different concerns and goals. In Singapore, such a structure has nurtured an environment where officials learn to have *fights* that are productive and which generate critical thinking, based on rational thinking and analyses. Before Singapore's Mass Rapid Transit (MRT) system was approved, former Deputy Prime Minister Goh Keng Swee encouraged a rigorous, decade-long debate on the alternatives:

> *[Goh Keng Swee] objected to the MRT because the case for having the MRT was that "you have no alternative"... That's not to say he objected to the MRT but he objected to the logic, which is not a frivolous matter. He objected to people who don't think deeply enough and argued deeply enough. That was what he was after.*[7]
>
> *Lim Siong Guan, former head of Civil Service*

These robust discussions, while sometimes heated, have eventually led to better collective decisions on planning and implementation. Trade-offs made among the three liveability outcomes are then better understood by all parties and appropriately managed. Such *productive fights* within the government have been supported by a Cabinet that is collaborative, with diverse experience across different portfolios, serving as the final conflict arbitrator.

Principle 3: Build in some flexibility

Singapore's city planners accept that no plan was perfect as the future is ultimately unpredictable. Consequently, the Concept Plan has been

---

[7] Lim Siong Guan, interview by the Centre for Liveable Cities, Singapore, 26 November 2012. Lim is currently group president of GIC Private Limited. He held previous appointments as head of Civil Service and permanent secretary at the Ministry of Finance and the Prime Minister's Office; he was also chairman of the Economic Development Board, among other posts.

periodically reviewed in the light of changing conditions, such as shifts in the economic or social environment:

> *We cannot be so rigid that what was planned has to be executed without any adjustment. We can't. If so, then there [would have been] no business parks. If so, there is no 'One North'.*[8]
>
> *Tan Chin Nam, former managing director, Economic Development Board*

The government has also been open to changing the schedule or form of certain developments lined up in the Master Plan. For instance Sungei Buloh, slated to become an agro-technology park, was instead turned into a wetland reserve in 1989, given that there was no pressing need for the area to be developed.[9]

Some other land parcels are also reserved for future use and zoned in a way that gives developers some leeway in the land use mix, a concept known as 'white sites': the Marina Bay area[10] is a prominent example.

Principle 4: Execute effectively

A plan is only as good as its successful implementation. In Singapore, the coordinated efforts of the operational agencies set up to implement policies and programmes have been key.

---

[8] Tan Chin Nam, interview by the Centre for Liveable Cities, Singapore, 21 February 2012. Tan is currently chairman of the Media Development Authority. He has held previous public sector appointments, including managing director of the Economic Development Board and permanent secretary in various ministries.

'One North' refers to a cluster of world-class research facilities and business park space, built to support the growth of biomedical sciences, physical sciences, Infocomm Technology, media and engineering.

[9] S Dhanabalan, interview by the Centre for Liveable Cities, Singapore, 20 December 2011.

[10] John Keung, interview by the Centre for Liveable Cities, Singapore, 27 July 2011. Keung, who is currently chief executive officer of the Building and Construction Authority (BCA), among other appointments, had held posts as deputy CEO (Building) of the Housing and Development Board and other senior planning posts in Singapore's urban development agencies.

One important element of effective execution is the careful preparation that takes place before implementation, including extensive research into the situation at hand. This was the case when Singapore first introduced its 'new town' concept:

> *I spent more than half a year to define what was a new town ... We wanted the new town to be highly self-sufficient, as highly self-sufficient as a new town can afford. So I interviewed a lot of people ... all kinds of people, industries and so on. ... Basically the question is how many people do you need to sustain an emporium, to sustain a supermarket, to sustain a polyclinic etc. And the number came to 250,000.*[11]
>
> *Liu Thai Ker former CEO, Housing and Development Board and Urban Redevelopment Authority and chairman, Centre for Liveable Cities*

Executing a plan is also not just about completing the project but giving careful consideration to the maintenance of what has been built. For instance, the upkeep and upgrading of existing sewage systems in Singapore has proven much more cost effective than digging up and replacing the old structures.

Principle 5: Innovate systematically

Urban development will always face resource limits, whether natural, physical or financial. However, innovation can mitigate these limits and, in some cases, overcome them in the long term. Solving Singapore's urban problems has required officials to be able to see different possibilities beyond the conventional wisdom; in some cases, they have to dare to dream big: Singapore's Deep Tunnel Sewerage System[12] and

---

[11] Liu Thai Ker, interview by the Centre for Liveable Cities, Singapore, 16 September 2011.

[12] The Deep Tunnel Sewerage System is conceptualised and managed by the PUB, Singapore's national water agency. It will process Singapore's used water collection, treatment, reclamation and disposal through deep tunnel pipes. For full information, visit <http://www.pub.gov.sg/dtss/Pages/default.aspx> accessed 17 September 2015.

Semakau landfill (which is environmentally conscious and now visited by nature lovers) are notable examples.

Innovation can also come in the form of policies. In 1998, Singapore became the first country to introduce an electronic road pricing system to manage traffic congestion; in 2000, it implemented a marginal cost pricing system for water. These bold policies have been attributed to the 'high level of administrative innovation' present in the government.[13]

Dynamic urban governance

The best intentions in planning amount to nothing if a city's urban governance system — or lack of one — does not allow good plans to be crafted and realised. Sound urban governance creates the right conditions for a city to achieve its liveable city outcomes.

Singapore's urban governance has been distinguished by its efficient provision of basic services to citizens and the establishment of competent institutions for development and coordination. Its geographical scale and structure of government has allowed for efficiency in policy formation and implementation, and the country has been able to achieve economic and institutional development. At the same time, Singapore's size and lack of resources has made it perennially vulnerable to changes in the external political and economic environment.

In this context, Singapore had had to evolve an urban governance approach that is dynamic, allowing its leaders to make optimal decisions and choices in an unpredictable, complex and constantly changing environment as well as helping society develop the capacity to deal with challenging situations.

Of the many elements that constitute Singapore's approach to dynamic urban governance, five have stood out as implicit principles.

---

[13] Lim Hng Kiang, interview by the Centre for Liveable Cities, Singapore, 13 April 2012. Lim, who is currently minister for Trade and Industry, was previously minister for National Development.

Principle 1: Lead with vision and pragmatism

How leadership is exercised both at the political and bureaucratic levels has an important impact on planning and implementation. A leadership with vision and political will to realise it has been critical for Singapore's development. Of particular importance was the political will to push through policies or projects that were considered unpopular or politically difficult at the time, but which were for the long-term benefit of the country and its people. For instance, the government's spate of land acquisitions from the late 1960s was regarded as somewhat draconian, but deemed necessary for Singapore's subsequent development:

> *If you go back and think of some of the things that were done ... How land acquisitions were carried out in those days cannot be done today. But it had to be done in those days ... [What is required is] a strong political will and a population that recognises that this has to be done.*[14]
>
> *Mah Bow Tan, former Cabinet minister*

Principle 2: Build a culture of integrity

Since Singapore's independence, a culture of integrity has been enforced by governance systems that stress the importance of accountability, transparency and incorruptibility. This culture of integrity has affected how Singapore's public officers, as well as politicians, carry out their responsibilities, earning them a high degree of credibility and legitimacy:

> *You must have the governance right. Once you have corruption, bad administration, fickle decision making, which can be influenced by friendship or favours or bribes, then you've got a problem.*[15]
>
> *Lee Kuan Yew, former prime minister*

---

[14] Mah Bow Tan, interview by the Centre for Liveable Cities, Singapore, 30 November 2011. Mah held previous appointments as minister for National Development, minister for Communications and minister for the Environment.

[15] Lee Kuan Yew, interview by Asit Biswas and Cecilia Tortajada, 11 February 2009.

The government has taken pains to inculcate a sense of accountability in public officers. City planners are responsible for large infrastructure projects that shape the city and the daily lives of citizens, from the roads used to the roofs over their heads. The government has had to ensure that sound financing mechanisms are put in place to maintain fiscal solvency and the sustainability of the projects:

> *We are very proud of the fact that we don't borrow money. Not even for development. This leads to very, very tight rules on budgeting, which is good. You can say it is good for budget discipline ... in Singapore, we kept ourselves bound to what we are able to earn, and pay for everything.*[16]
>
> *Lim Siong Guan, former head of Civil Service*

Principle 3: Cultivate sound institutions

Strong institutions with well thought-out systems and processes contribute to better decision making, leading to more effective planning and development. Singapore's approach has been to use a range of structures (both formal and informal) in planning and to allow these structures to evolve as the situation requires. Aside from formal institutions, less formal norms of governance have also been important, such as a rational approach to policy, respect for sound professional competence and meritocracy.

Professionalism is an important feature in Singapore's public institutions. Many professional bureaucrats are technical experts as well as strategists who are well able to defend their ideas when necessary.

The separation of politics and the professional services, as embodied in Singapore's institutions, is another significant norm. While politicians focused on strategy and policy, the professional and technical issues are handled by the agencies, leading to greater accountability and effectiveness. At the same time, mutual respect between the political

[16] Lim Siong Guan, interview by the Centre for Liveable Cities, Singapore, 26 November 2012.

leadership and the bureaucracy contributes to better decisions and clarity of action and responsibility. This was evident, for instance, in the decade-long clean-up of the Singapore River, beginning in 1977:

> *The technical engineering problems, we deal with, we don't get interference from Members of Parliament, politicians saying, "Why don't you do this?" They don't tell us how to clean up. We deal with that part. But the social and political problems, being the elected government and [having] practically all the seats in Parliament, they had the political will and political muscle to carry though all these things.*[17]
>
> *Lee Ek Tieng, former head of Civil Service*

Institutional rules and norms, both formal and informal, have enabled government agencies to work effectively together, irrespective of different or competing interests or professional opinions.

Principle 4: Involve the community as stakeholders

Creating a liveable city is a huge and complex undertaking, and city planners need the support of the city's inhabitants for projects and policies to succeed and to be sustainable. No government has all the answers or inexhaustible resources. Creating a stake in the city for the community provides opportunities for the public, people and private sectors to work together for the long-term good of the city.

The Singapore government has increasingly involved the community in protecting the country's shared resources, as well as in the policy-forming process. While policy and planning decisions are fundamentally undertaken by the government, public engagement enhances the legitimacy of decision-making and policy outcomes. When Chek Jawa, a biodiversity-rich area, was slated for development, the Nature Society

[17] Lee Ek Tieng and Tan Gee Paw, interview by Asit Biswas and Cecilia Tortajada, Singapore, 9 February 2011. Lee was former head of Singapore's Civil Service.

(Singapore)[18] lobbied the government to preserve the area. The result was a reprieve in 2002:

> *I feel that NParks and Nature Society worked very well together because of our improved relations ... We did agree not to do too much confrontational fighting with the government on Chek Jawa ... The really important thing was that the public supported it, and other groups started up spontaneously to support it.*[19]
>
> *Geh Min, former president of Nature Society (Singapore)*

When the government and key community stakeholders work together for the greater public good, the result is a collective win for the country.

Principle 5: Work with markets

A key governance principle and a fiscally prudent approach have been to harness market forces to improve efficiency.

The private sector has played a part in the provision of services where the government alone could not provide, or services which the government wanted to relinquish in order to re-direct public funds to different priorities. The government has also successfully privatised power generation and some parts of public transportation. This approach has enabled the government to implement a wide range of programmes more effectively.

[18] The Nature Society (Singapore) is a non-government, non-profit organisation dedicated to the appreciation, conservation, study and enjoyment of the natural heritage in Singapore, Malaysia and the surrounding regions. It was formerly known as the Singapore branch of the Malayan Nature Society. The branch was formed in 1954 and renamed Nature Society (Singapore) in 1991.

[19] Geh Min, interview by the Centre for Liveable Cities, Singapore, 14 March 2012. Geh was former president of the Nature Society (Singapore) and a board member of The Nature Conservancy's Asia Pacific Council and the Singapore Environment Council. She was a nominated member of parliament from 2005 to 2006.

Nevertheless, there are limits to private sector involvement in the provision of public services. The government has had to be clear about the kind of services that cannot be outsourced or privatised, given the overall role and responsibility of the government. In the case of Surbana Corporation Pte Ltd, which used to be HDB's Building and Development Division and is now an international building consultant, the issue of maintaining control is clear:

> *Surbana is a good positive example where the expertise we have garnered by building public housing in Singapore can now be applied elsewhere. We can sell these services but we still have to be clear that Surbana should still be controlled by us [Temasek Holdings, the Singapore government's investment vehicle] because they have a big role to play in Singapore.*[20]
>
> *S Dhanabalan, former Cabinet minister*

Conclusion

The principles of the CLC Liveability Framework, distilled from a study of Singapore's unique urban development experience, are not meant to be exhaustive. Instead, it seeks to outline some general principles that underpin effective urban planning and governance, considering urbanisation issues from strategic, managerial and political perspectives, not just from purely technical ones.

The Framework could provide some useful insights to cities interested in raising and sustaining their liveability standards with the approach that best suits their particular circumstances.

As part of Singapore's efforts to share its experience, as well as to learn from other cities CLC co-organises the biennial Lee Kuan Yew World City Prize for outstanding contributions towards liveable and sustainable communities. Prize laureates include Bilbao in 2010, New York City in 2012 and Suzhou in 2014. To promote learning and sharing among city leaders, CLC also plays host to the annual World

---

[20] S Dhanabalan, interview by the Centre for Liveable Cities, Singapore, 20 December 2011.

Cities Summit Mayors Forum — the largest gathering of city leaders in the world.

> *We learn what not to do by watching other cities and also what to do from watching good cities. There is nothing new that you can think of that has not been tried by thousands of other cities.*[21]
>
> *Lee Kuan Yew, former prime minister*

[21] Lee Kuan Yew, interview by the Centre for Liveable Cities, Singapore, 31 August 2012.

Chapter 2

Singapore's Approach to Urban Planning

John WONG and ZHAO Litao*

Introduction

Singapore is both a city and a state. It has achieved a high level of economic and social development in spite of its small size and physical constraints. An equally impressive achievement is high liveability amidst high density and rapid economic growth. Despite a population growth of 68% between 1986 and 2007, Singapore's green cover increased from 36% to 47%.[1]

Many factors help account for Singapore's transformation from a third world country to a first world one, and from a city with one of the largest urban ghettoes in Southeast Asia to a highly liveable cosmopolitan city well connected to the world. Urban planning, a technical and political process to balance competing needs for scarce land, undoubtedly has its place among the contributing factors. Singapore's

*John WONG is Professorial Fellow and academic adviser to the East Asian Institute of the National University of Singapore. ZHAO Litao is Senior Research Fellow of the same institute.

[1] Peter Ho, *The Planning of A City-State*, Working Paper Series, no. 2, 2013, Lee Kuan Yew Centre for Innovative Cities.

experience in using urban planning to achieve economic and social development and to make the city liveable can be valuable lessons to cities with similar aspirations.

In this chapter, we briefly introduce the evolution of urban planning in Singapore and the main instruments utilised. As Singapore develops, urban planning takes on new tasks and challenges. Innovative solutions become critical as population growth puts even greater pressure on city planners and managers. Some of the new developments and some unique features of Singapore's urban planning will also be highlighted.

Evolution of urban planning in Singapore

Shortly after Singapore was founded as a British colony in 1819 by Stamford Raffles, the British rulers embarked on rudimentary city planning, zoning different parts of the Singapore island for different uses, such as the civic district for trade and commerce, and different settlements for different ethnic groups of the Chinese, the Indians and the Malays. Today, distinctive ethnic enclaves like Chinatown, Little India and Kampong Glam and the Central Business District have lingering traces of the early colonial period.

Singapore emerged from World War II and the Japanese occupation in great physical ruin and destruction, and serious housing shortages became pronounced in the post-war period. Slums and overcrowding were the major urban problems throughout the 1950s.

The present ruling People's Action Party (PAP) came to power in 1959 when Singapore gained self-government. The PAP government quickly set up the Housing Development Board (HDB) as a statutory body to provide public housing, along with the Economic Development Board (EDB) for promoting Singapore's industrialisation. HDB has since become a major player in Singapore's subsequent urban plans.

Singapore started with more systematic urban planning after its independence in 1965, with urban planning also becoming more purposeful and highly development-oriented. Politically, urban planning was part of Singapore's overall nation-building efforts. Economically and socially, urban planning was also one of the key components of the

Singapore model of economic development, with the government playing an active and central role. This is commonly called East Asian 'development state model'.

Over the past four decades, a number of landmark development projects had figured prominently in Singapore's urban planning process, including Jurong Town (a thriving industrial estate converted from a swamp), the building of Changi International Airport from reclaimed land, the creation of Marina South based on large-scale land reclamation and more recently, the extension of water catchment areas and the building of Marina Barrage for raising Singapore's level of water self-sufficiency.

Over the years, most urban planning efforts were concentrated on the creation of new towns, which grew hand in hand with the expansion of public housing. In fact, the public housing programme was planned in such a way that its expansion was closely linked to the creation of fully planned new towns: Queenstown, Toa Payoh, Ang Mo Kio, Marine Parade, Tampines, Jurong East and West, Punggol, Yishun, Woodlands and so on.

In 1974, the Urban Redevelopment Authority (URA) was created as a statutory board and became the main agency for Singapore's urban planning, taking charge of national land use planning and conservation, urban renewal, land sales and development control. Above all, URA was charged with drawing up Singapore's two main instruments of urban planning: (i) The Concept Plan; and (ii) The Master Plan.

Early phases of urban planning were much influenced by the fundamental needs of fostering economic growth and employment generation, and social stability and harmony. Subsequently, as Singapore develops, urban planning goes for the modern features that constitute a liveable city, paying more attention to conservation, heritage sites, green buildings and the like.

Apart from national development objectives, Singapore's urban planning has been distinctly influenced by some of Lee Kuan Yew's personal traits and strategic thinking, such as his idea of a "garden city", his obsession with cleanliness, orderliness, a corruption-free public administration, and social mobility and social equity. He was also very keen to reduce Singapore's dependency on water supply from Malaysia, which has profoundly shaped Singapore's policy towards water catchment areas and water technology. Many of his ideas have greatly shaped the direction and focus of Singapore's urban planning.[2]

The concept plan and the master plan

As Singapore is a small city state with a land area of over 700 square kilometres, the main challenge is to plan the scarce land for different uses such as housing, industry, recreation, infrastructure, water catchment and military in a more "optimal manner". The end objective is to provide inhabitants with a secure and a comfortable living environment.

Hence there is a need for a "Concept Plan" (CP) to take a long-term view to ensure enough land to meet future population and economic growth with a good-quality, liveable environment. The CP is a strategic land use and transportation plan for the next 40 to 50 years, revised every 10 years to keep pace with demographic, economic, social and technological changes. Prepared by the URA, it has to go through a long process of review and extensive public consultation and feedback. The CP has since gone through several rounds of revisions.

First Concept Plan, 1971. Prepared with advice from UN experts, it adopted the "Ring Concept Plan", which envisages the development of a string of new towns radiating from the central business district (CBD) and water catchment areas, with each town separated by green spaces but linked up by an island-wide system of expressways and mass rapid transit (MRT). Subsequently, many new towns were built along this overall concept. This 1971 plan was to cater to the long-term population growth of up to four million.

1974–1989 Central Area Plans. This period focused on the development or the re-development of the Central Area, which was historically the hub of Singapore's commercial and banking activities. The URA was set up in 1974 to redevelop many old sites in the central district and resettle residents affected by redevelopment.

---

[2] Peter Ho, *The Planning of A City-State.*

In 1983, URA came out with an urban design plan for the orderly transformation of the CBD, promoting high-rise office buildings while conserving some historical and heritage old buildings in between these buildings. The 1989 Conservation Plan went further by designating historic districts like Chinatown, Little India, Kampong Glam and the Singapore River (Boat Quay and Clarke Quay) for conservation-cum-development.

1991 Concept Plan. By 1990, much of Singapore's basic infrastructure, new towns, expressways, MRT, CBD renewal etc had already been in place. The main thrust of new development was contained in the new slogan, "Towards a Tropical City of Excellence". In other words, the main emphasis was how to fine-tune achievements of previous Plans and to go for better quality of life and stronger Singapore identity.

2001 Concept Plan. Under the title of "Towards a Thriving World Class City for the 21st Century", this CP mapped out a long-term vision for urban development for the next 40–50 years, based on the population scenario of 5.5 million. Key proposals include new housing in familiar places, high-rise city living but a room with a view, more choices for recreation, greater flexibility for business, a global business centre, extensive rail networks and focus on identity. This plan was to prepare Singapore for the 21st century by embracing greater globalisation and opening up more to foreigners — foreign talents and foreign workers.

2011 Concept Plan. This is the ongoing plan, which has been under extensive review since 2010. It was originally planned for a population of seven million. In 2012, the government published a White Paper on Population, which was put under the same process of public consultation and public feedback. However, the public reacted negatively to the new "population policy". The population debate sparked off an anti-foreigner backlash. The PAP government clarified that population projections beyond 2020 are not targets but meant for infrastructure planning. It nevertheless tightened the policy towards foreign workers, and succeeded in preventing the population issue from becoming a hot-button issue again in the 2015 General Election.

The Master Plan (MP) is the statutory land use plan to guide Singapore's actual urban development for the next 10 to 15 years. The MP is supposed to translate the broad goals and objectives of the CP into a detailed and workable land use guide. Whereas the CP is full of ideas and conceptual details, the MP is full of operational details. Unlike the CP, the MP has "legal teeth" for implementation. It is the most important policy tool that shapes Singapore's physical development because it controls the pattern of land use and land-use density. The MP depends on the collaboration of various government agencies for implementation.

After its independence, Singapore had its first MP in 1985, which had been revised and amended eight times. The current 2008 MP is supposed to incorporate the ideas, strategies and policies of all the CPs.

The MP controls and regulate urban development in several ways.

Zoning — how different parts of the city are demarcated for residential, residential-cum-commercial, commercial, hotel, open space, sports and recreation, roads, health-care, educational institution, place of worship, community and civic centre, park, cemetery and so on.

Plot ratio — the maximum permissible intensity for developments within the demarcated area.

Building height plan — height controls operate with gross plot ratio: for instance, a gross plot ratio of 1.4 will allow a five-storey height and a gross plot ratio of 1.6 will allow a 12-storey height.

Landed housing area plan — some residential estates are designated as mixed housing (i.e. landed property, semi-detached etc.) while others are designated as good class bungalow area, with strict plot ratio and height controls.

Besides, there are Activity Generating Uses Plans for shops and food outlets, and plans for parks and open spaces, conservation areas and monuments.

In summary, the MP controls development through zoning, plot ratio and height controls, and moderates and regulates development through imposing "development charges" and development levies. Required by government statutes, any development within demarcated area is subject to payment of development charge or temporary development levy. Finally, two more factors operate to strengthen effectiveness of urban planning and empower the government's role in urban planning: (i) most lands in Singapore are owned by the government, as part of the colonial legacies — the "crown land". Private ownership of land is divided into freehold and leasehold. (ii) In 1966, the Land Acquisition Act was passed, allowing the government to acquire any land for public uses (infrastructure) by compensation based on current value and zoning. Landowners may question the compensation value, but not the acquisition, i.e. the acquisition is compulsory. In other countries, acquisition and compensation involve prolonged legal disputes, expensive and time consuming. Singapore by and large avoids such problems.

Some new developments

As Singapore develops, urban planning faces the challenge of rising demands and aspirations. Innovative solutions are needed to meet higher expectations. Economically, urban planning has an important role to play in industrial upgrading and economic restructuring. Over the years, Singapore has made plans to phase out or rejuvenate older industrial estates, develop technology corridors near research universities and regional centres and reclaim offshore areas for the expanded CBD.[3]

As Singapore becomes more developed and affluent, the housing aspirations of Singaporeans have changed as well. In the earlier days when housing shortage was an acute problem, the priority of HDB was to build flats as quickly as possible, without much regard for design and other features. With the growth of middle-class families, who demand larger and better HDB flats, the HDB has adjusted its priority from building smaller flats (1-room, 2-room or 3-room) to building larger flats and upgrading the existing estates. Progressively, community amenities such as sports and swimming complex and shops were added.

[3] Centre for Liveable City and Civil Service College, *Liveable and Sustainable Cities: A Framework*, 2014, <http://www.clc.gov.sg/documents/books/CLC_CSC Liveable&SustainableCities.pdf> accessed 30 July 2014.

Premium flats with enhanced features comparable to private flats were also offered to better off families. Today, Singapore has to simultaneously deal with three generations of estates: the older ones, the middle-aged ones and new ones. It now makes plans to realise the vision of new estates, rejuvenate the middle-aged estates and regenerate older estates.

Higher demands for recreation and conservation of heritage are also a result of development. Singapore's response includes the provision of parks and recreation areas that would be well distributed across the island, the development of riverine parks, the preservation of nature reserves and the conservation of built heritage.

The creative use of space is critical to a city-state like Singapore. Singapore has tried to make space work harder for different uses, by building walking and cycling tracks along canals and drains, establishing lifestyle and leisure outlets along underground walkways linking train stations and buildings, turning rooftop spaces into sky gardens, swimming pools and tourist attractions, cleaning up rivers and changing them into water catchments and so on.

Ensuring self-sufficiency in water supply is part of Singapore's urban planning. Apart from the NEWater project, which produces high-grade reclaimed water, Singapore has been expanding the water catchment area to eventually cover 90% of the land area. Canals and drains have been turned into water catchments, while high pollution control standards are employed to prevent contamination of Singapore's water resources with the expansion of industrial and residential estates into the water catchment areas.[4]

To make the city highly liveable in spite of high density, Singapore has developed community spatial designs to boost neighbourhood watch and allow for greater connectivity through an island-wide network of nature reserves, parks, Park Connector Network, easily accessible treetop walks, a greener city through the concept of "Pervasive Greenery" (to the pavement, flyover, building façade and rooftop), the

---

[4]Centre for Liveable City and Civil Service College, *Liveable and Sustainable Cities: A Framework*.

project of Active, Beautiful, Clean Waters and green technology and standards.

Some unique features of Singapore's urban planning

Singapore is both a city and an independent state. Urban planning is the same as national development planning. Thus, Singapore can have an effective public housing programme catering to 85% of the population, much like a "land reform in a city". The homeownership programme is not planned as a welfare provision to the low-income population. It is first and foremost a political project meant to make every Singaporean a stakeholder in the survival and growth of a young country without a long history and facing a lot of uncertainties.[5] Such a programme is not possible in other cities with vast hinterland and an unlimited supply of rural migrants.

Singapore's urbanisation is basically an "endogenous process" without uncontrolled rural migration as in other cities. Small and compact and without a rural hinterland, urban planning is relatively easy to execute.

Singapore has a strong government, with very little political opposition. Consensus could be obtained easily and CP and MP are not as extensively politicised as they would in countries that are polarised by political processes.

Above all, Singapore has good governance with an efficient civil service, which is free from corruption. This is backed by an effective legal system. So plans are not shelved for lack of implementation as in other developing countries.

As is the case for every city, there are limits to how far urban planning can go. Urban planning can be unduly influenced by the zeitgeist (the spirit of the time) thinking. At every period of time, certain popu-

[5] Zhao Litao and John Wong, "Singapore's Social Development Experience: A Relevant Lesson for China?", in Zhao Litao (ed.) *China's Social Development and Policy*, London, Routledge, 2013, pp. 230–252.

lar values or certain fads and fashions could dominate thinking and behaviour, which may later prove to be just fickle and not enduring.

No plan can adequately address future uncertainty caused particularly by rapid and unforeseen technological change. An old plan made 10 years ago may have failed to capture the main thrust of today's globalisation process, or some drastic changes in human interaction and behaviour caused by the internet and the social media. Even the Club of Rome had predicted wrongly in the early 1970s on the energy issue. As technological progress is always full of surprises, whether planners can predict future social behaviour is still an unknown. What awaits is possibly a future full of game-changing events.

Chapter 3

Urbanisation in Vietnam: Behind the Successful Façade

PHAM Thuy Loan*

Overview of Urbanisation in Vietnam

Country Profile

Vietnam, officially named the Socialist Republic of Vietnam is the easternmost country on the Indochina Peninsula in Southeast Asia. With an estimated 90 million inhabitants as of 2013, it is the world's 13th most populous country, and the eighth most populous Asian country. The country is bordered by China to the north, Laos to the north-west, Cambodia to the south-west, and the South China Sea to the east.

Vietnam covers a total area of approximately 331,210 square kilometres (127,881 square miles), making it almost the size of Germany and 65th largest in the world in terms of land area. The combined length of the country's land boundaries is 4,639 kilometres (2,883 miles), and its coastline is 3,444 kilometres (2,140 miles) long. By 2013, 32% of the population are now living in urban area, and the annual urbanisation rate is about 3.5%. Vietnam's gross domestic

* Pham Thuy Loan is Deputy Director at the Vietnam National Institute of Architecture in the Ministry of Construction, Vietnam.

product (GDP) was US$170.02 billion in 2013 and ranked 58th globally. Its per capita income at US$1,895.576 was ranked 134th globally, implying that Vietnam was out of the list of low-income countries since 2009.

Urbanisation trends

Since the 1986 Doi Moi reforms, Vietnam's urbanisation started to accelerate. The country has experienced two major transitions: first, the demographic transition from rural to urban that has expedited the urbanisation process; and second, economic transition from the centrally planned to market-oriented economy. Vietnam's urban population has begun to grow since the late 1990s, indicating that urbanisation has transitioned from incipient to intermediate stage with rapid urbanisation (currently 35% of Vietnam's population is urban, with an annual urban population growth of 3.5%) as its economy increasingly oriented towards industrial manufacturing as a share of both employment and economic output.

It should be noted that Vietnam's overall urbanisation progressed at a similar stage as China, India and Indonesia until the late 1970s when it slowed down as did China and Indonesia (Figure 1). However, the United Nations' projection in 2008 suggests that country's urban population will continue to increase for the next two decades and exceed the rural population by 2040.

Vietnam urban classification and the evolving urban system

Vietnam currently has 765 cities, towns and townships, classified into six classes according to the Decree 42/2009/ND-CP of the Government of Vietnam on urban classification (Figure 2). The urban classification system is hierarchically classified into six classes of urban areas defined by different levels of economic significance, physical development, population, population density and infrastructure provision. There is a large gap between Special-class cities or Class I cities and Class VI,

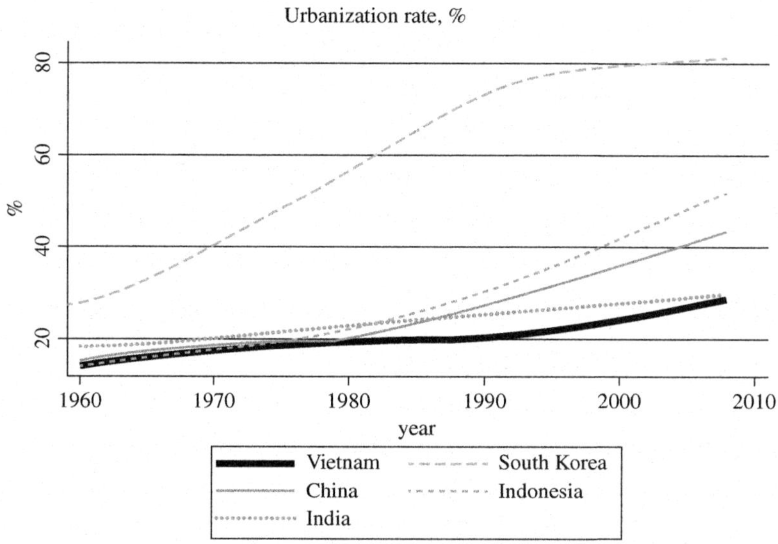

Figure 1. Urbanisation Rate in Vietnam (%)

Source: World Bank, World Development Indicators.

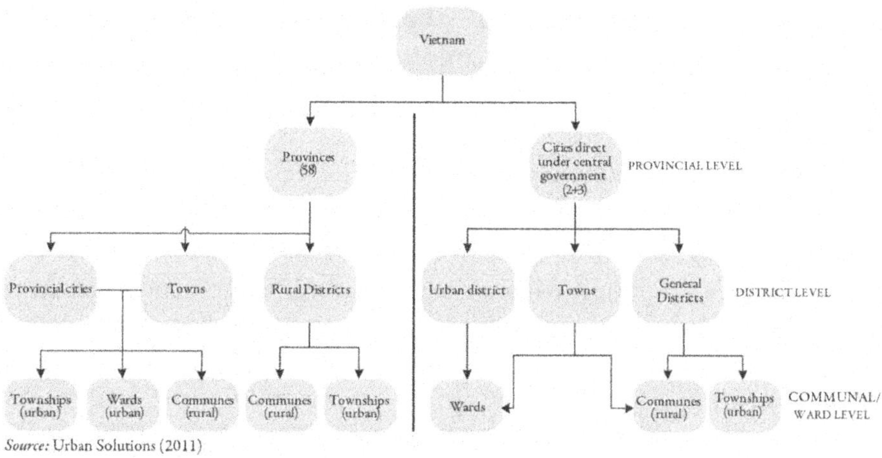

Figure 2. Urban Classification System in Vietnam

Source: Urban Solutions, "Urban Evolution", *Vietnam Urbanization Review background papers,* World Bank, 2011.

Class V urban areas/townships. The Decree 42/2009/ND-CP categorises a Class V township as one that has a population of 4,000 people, population density of about 2,000 people per square kilometre, and 65% of the population working in non-agricultural sector. Special-class cities, on the other hand, must have a population of more than five million. By 2014, Vietnam has two special cities, 15 Class I cities, 19 Class II cities, 43 Class III towns, 67 Class IV provincial towns and 619 Class V small townships.

The average city size in 2009 and its growth between 1999 and 2009 show a distinct core-periphery structural pattern.

Vietnam has developed Ho Chi Minh City and Hanoi into two independent and dominant core-periphery urban systems. The two special-class cities are located in the centre of two economic agglomerations in the north and the south. Ho Chi Minh City's and Hanoi's "special" status can be attributed to their significant and unique economic and political contributions to the country.

Vietnam's rapid economic growth is driven by these two urban systems with high growth and industrial concentration within these cities and their surrounding areas. The finding that economic growth is led by a single or a few core economic nodes is consistent with the experience of other rapidly developing countries in incipient or intermediate stages of urbanisation.

Da Nang is strategically chosen as a key economic growth pole and designated to function as such for the central region. However, Da Nang's city growth is mainly driven by in-situ urbanisation (i.e. short-distance migration within the same administrative boundaries or rural-urban land conversion). It is unlikely that Da Nang will grow to play a pivotal role in the national urban system, as Hanoi or Ho Chi Minh City does.

The current administrative system of urban areas and the urban classification system provide incentives for cities and towns to move up the urban class ladder. Striving for higher classification standards has in recent years become a major preoccupation of local government authorities as urban areas of higher classes receive greater recognition and share of financial resources. "Cities often make investments in infrastructure to enable them to meet the requirements of the next classification level, rather than in direct response to the immediate needs of the population. For example, a city or town may invest in road expansion when there is only limited traffic demand, instead of expanding piped water supply, where clear need exists."[1] Cities sometimes enlarge their administrative boundary outward to include surrounding rural settlements and lands to meet the population size requirement. Many cities do not meet most of the specified criteria in the higher classification, yet are allowed to delay. The current system has in fact resulted in fake records of urbanisation in many regions, ineffective investments in many cities, resources wastage and rapid loss of agricultural lands around cities and town.

Welfare and urban services

While Vietnam's economic development is concentrated in the two core metropolitan regions of Ho Chi Minh City and Hanoi as expected, welfare improvements have been more widespread countrywide. Overall, there appears to be strong convergence of welfare across provinces. The welfare improvement is mainly driven by the government's strong continuous commitment to inclusive social development, and underpinned economically by the strong growth of core metropolitan cities and ensuing positive spillover to the hinterlands. These improvements must be interpreted with caution and viewed in perspective. Disparities in accessibility to and quality of services remain and there are areas of persistent poverty in Vietnam. Vietnam, like many countries, has advanced from the incipient to intermediate stage of urbanisation and from lower- to middle-income society. It therefore needs to take into consideration not only the accessibility of basic services but also the quality and reliability.

---

[1] A. Coulhart, N. Quang and H. Sharp, *Urban Development Strategy: Meeting the Challenges of Rapid Urbanization and the Transition to Market Oriented Economy*, Hanoi, World Bank Office in Vietnam, 2006.

Key features and phases of Vietnamese urbanisation strategy

As Vietnam enters a crucial period of urbanisation corresponding to its present stage of economic development, the Vietnamese government has placed strong emphasis on developing its system of cities. This commitment is explicitly stated by Deputy Prime Minister Nguyen Sinh Hung at the Vietnam National Urban Conference held from 6 to 7 November 2009: "Vietnam will have only one chance to get urbanisation right. If we fail at urbanisation, we will fail at industrialisation and modernisation."

Although Vietnam has embarked on a trajectory of rapid economic liberalisation with the inception of Doi Moi, its government has also implemented a variety of policies to foster a more even distribution of economic growth and urban development.

Achievements, problems and challenges

Urban housing development

After the implementation of the Doi Moi policy, Vietnam's real estate market materialised, turning housing and land into tradeable as well as the most profitable commodity. Vietnam has adopted three major models of housing provision: state-provided (before the Doi-moi), self-reliant (by individuals) and commercial. Large cities in Vietnam have created a pluralistic supply of housing to meet the needs of different segments of population.

As a lower-income and rapidly urbanising country, Vietnam has relatively few urban slums. Vietnam has a permissive, accepting and sometimes proactive regulatory approach towards customary and affordable housing development. This, coupled with the innovative small-scale private housing construction and rental sector, has resulted in a very low incidence of slums in Vietnamese cities. This is particularly striking compared with cities in countries with higher urban incomes than Vietnam (such as India, the Philippines, Indonesia and Brazil, to mention a few).

Table 1. Government Policies to Control and Guide Urban Development in Vietnam.

Urban Development Policies	**Consequences**
Central Control of Administrative Boundary Shifts	From 1954 to the present, administrative boundary changes required approval from the central government. This has historically been viewed as an effective tool for controlling city size and encroachment of urban areas onto agricultural lands. However, with pressure of urbanisation since Doi Moi policy in the late 1980s, and more recently, driven by political will of local government, many cities have extended their boundaries, resulting in an increased loss of agricultural land to urban use and exacerbating conflicts at the urban fringe of many cities.
Controlling Population Movements and the Demographic Transition	The demographic transition has been largely controlled by the urban residency permission system, which is essentially a Vietnamese version of the Chinese *hukou* system. This was considered largely effective for its intended purpose from 1954 to 1990. Since 1990 this policy has been relaxed — the effects of which can be seen in the demographic transition since 1990; the urban population rose from 19.5% in 1990 to roughly 30% in 2009 and to 35% in 2014. However, remnants of this system may result in an undercount of the actual urban population with many migrants potentially not accounted for.
Urban Service Provision and the Welfare Transition	From 1954 to the early 1990s, uniform utility rates for the provision of urban services largely discouraged the provision of these services and thus impacted their quality. In most cases since the 1990s and the 2000s, reforms in service provision were implemented to allow for cost recovery in tariffs and a shift to commercial practices. This has brought positive impact on increasing accessibility to basic services across all urban classifications. Quality of services remains a problem though and there is a large disparity in quality between services provided privately and public services, especially in health care and education, resulting in increasing social inequality.
Urban Finance and the Economic Transition	Urban construction finance, from 1954 to the present, has been largely controlled through the state and redistribution of revenues on a per capita basis. This has impacted positively on equity between regions and urban areas. However, this centrally allocated budget is always not enough for many cities to invest in infrastructure to keep them competitive and in pace with demand. Land sales constitute a big component of local cities' self-raised revenues that cities have for infrastructure investments. There is growing debate nationally to create new rules for larger cities (e.g. the Law on the Capital City).

(*Continued*)

Table 1. *(Continued)*

Urban Development Policies	**Consequences**
Land Markets and the Physical Transition	Urban land markets were largely ignored from 1954 to the 1990s. The 1993 Land Law was a step forward to release land into the land and housing market. Conversion of farmland to urban use accelerated rapidly, although the process was chaotic due to low compliance of legally recognised land use rights and widespread informal transactions. The 2003 Land Law further grants the use of land as a collateral in business and as eligibility to compensation if land is acquired by the government for development. The Land Price Framework (generally lower than "market" rates by 30% to 70%) is intended to stimulate economic development. While it is considered successful in attracting real estate investment, it has resulted in land speculation and land conflicts. Land prices are marked up to benefit the state and property developers at the expense of the original land owners and by creating a de facto two-tiered land price system.
Transition towards Pro-Urban Policies?	The Government Decree No. 72 (2001) and Decree No. 42 (2009) established city and town classification requirements to distinguish between the roles of different cities. The classification system has implications for administrative functions, tax collection and state funding allocations. A possibly unintended consequence has been a trend for cities to exploit loopholes in the classification system to move up in the ranking. These moves are largely administrative and not necessarily based on the actual economic function of the cities. The Government Decision No. 10 (1998) on the Urban System and Development Strategy to 2020 called for the development of medium- and small-sized cities and containing the growth of the largest cities. By 2009, the Government Decision No. 445 that updated the 1998 Decision with a vision to 2050 accepts the possibility of megacities with population over 10 million. The current thinking is to develop a system of cities that will play a role in the country's urban economy. However, these decrees are non-binding and are seen merely as statements of intent. The 2011–2020 Socio Economic Development Strategy accepts de facto that urbanisation will be necessary to promote the country's goals of industrialisation and modernisation.

Source: Vietnam Urbanization Review — Technical Assistance Report, World Bank, 2011.

Market mechanism has gradually become dominant in Vietnam's housing provision during the past 20 years in terms of quantity and quality. Every year, Vietnam develops about 30 to 70 million square metres of total housing supply, mostly concentrated in Hanoi, Ho Chi Minh City and Da Nang, with provision of better-quality and designed housing of diverse types and sizes, integrated infrastructure, amenities and services and better landscaping. In 2011, development in Hanoi had resulted in a total supply of 35,500 units of apartments and about 37,000 units of villas and houses, of which 23,400 units were at the phase of sale-contract to customers and 14,000 at phase of investment. However, problems emerged in the housing market, such as an over-supply of high-end products, inflated high prices, speculative demand rather than real demand, the emergence of "phantom" market and housing estate, and the lack of supply for middle- and low-end markets. The year 2012 witnessed a severe economic depression and real estate market was in the doldrums due to the problems.

It is envisioned that the rate and scale of urbanisation in Vietnam's cities in the next 20 years will require a low-income housing strategy to prevent slums in the future. In addition, it is imperative to take immediate measures to fix the current defects of housing market.

Urban mobility

Vietnam's cities enjoy relatively good urban mobility, due largely to such features as:

- the universal use of motorcycles as the primary means of transportation;
- the characteristic mixed land use in Vietnamese cities (where live, work and play facilities are in close proximity) that reduce people's demand for moving;
- the prevalence of shophouses, where people live in the space above or behind their store or workplace.

Despite Vietnam's relatively good mobility, the growth of private vehicles in cities has made commuting and moving one of the most

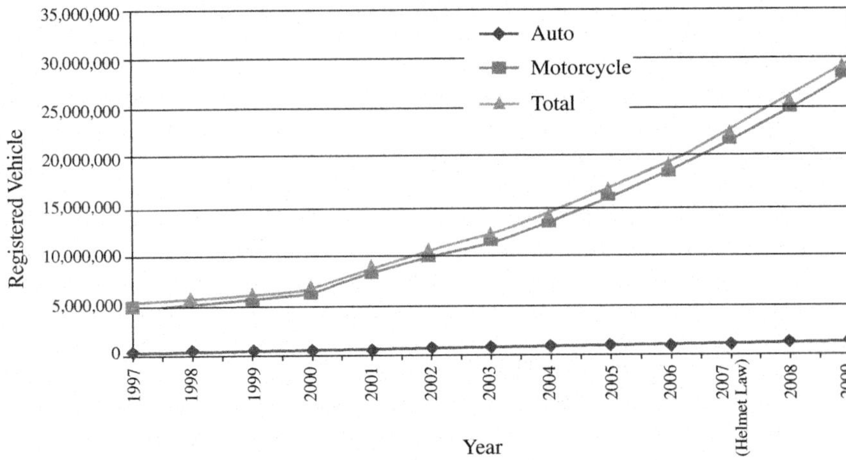

Figure 3. Number of Registered Vehicles in Vietnam, 1997–2009

Source: Ministry of Transport, Hanoi, Vietnam.

stressful daily activities. On the other hand, car population is expected to increase substantially in the coming years and the principal driving factor is the rising per capita income, as evident in most other countries. In Vietnam's largest cities, Hanoi and Ho Chi Minh City, the infrastructure is not capable of supporting extensive use of motor cars as the major means of transportation. Indeed, increased car use would eventually lead to traffic gridlock. The pattern of major streets in Hanoi is simply incompatible with the demand for road space created by a shift to private cars to even cater for a small fraction of the current trips made by motorcycles. With car ownership on the rise, while the benefits of planned transit systems are not yet reaped in coming 10 to 15 years, Vietnam's major challenge now and in the immediate years is to slow down the transition to automobiles.

While plans are in place to develop public transport system in most major cities, the preference of the majority Vietnamese for personal transport will run counter to plans of developing the urban transit systems. Therefore, public transport options should be designed as an integrated part of the system that incorporates the use of motorcycles and has a competitive edge over the car in overall cost and convenience.

In addition, market force and evolving land-use patterns in cities need to be taken into account in planning transit system.

Land management and governance

Land and real estate market regulations appear to be improving but more essential improvements have to be made. Enterprise survey data from two key surveys on Vietnamese firms conducted in 2005 and 2009 indicates substantial improvement in firms' accessibility to land use.

However, land markets in Vietnam reflect some of the deeper issues related to land management and governance. For instance, the huge discrepancies between the government's "set price" for land and the "market price", which is often 10 times higher than the "set price" have caused large distortions and bottlenecks in the land market. Also, since land allocations, joint venture deals, taxes, concessions and permissions for developers and investors are based on artificially deflated land values, the government has significantly jeopardised public interest by undervaluing its most valuable assets.

Urban planning system

Much of the master planning process in Vietnam is increasingly based on ideas rooted in physical design (not socio-economic realities). Spatial plans for Vietnamese cities remain heavily prescriptive with an emphasis on physical planning (i.e. creating cities "by design") and on permitted land uses — often down to ward or project level — without necessarily taking into account of the underlying socio-economic needs or market realities for that same city or area, which may be considerably more complex.

Functional fragmentation is an issue within (and across) spatial jurisdictions. In Vietnam, the socio-economic development plans (under the purview of departments of investment planning), land use plans (under the purview of departments of natural resources), urban master plans (under the purview of departments of construction), transport and infrastructure plans (under the purview of departments of transport and construction) and housing plans (under the purview of housing agencies under departments of construction) are typically not well coordinated with each other, or with the city-level administration. They are often implemented uncoordinated at different schedules and use inconsistent data and projections for planning. Functional fragmentation has thus posed a critical bottleneck to the planning process.

Concluding remarks and points to consider

According to the World Bank's assessment, Vietnam is widely considered a developmental success story. Driven by the Doi Moi reforms that began in 1986, Vietnam has rapidly evolved from one of the poorest countries in the world into an emerging middle-income country. In the span of about 25 years, its gross national income per capita has risen from less than US$100 to over US$1,000, living standards have tripled and the poverty headcount has fallen by 80%. With its accession to the World Trade Organization (WTO) in 2007, Vietnam has emerged as a global and regional powerhouse—international trade represented 160% of GDP; exports grew by 14% annually from 2006 to 2010; and many industrial exports have grown much faster.

The country's long-term development prospects are solid, but the sustainability of its growth will necessitate a shift from a reliance on low-cost labour and natural resources exploitation to a greater focus on productivity growth and technological advances while also ensuring greater macroeconomic stability. As Vietnam emerges as a middle-income country, its focus will necessarily shift to addressing sustainability, quality and equity of growth while tackling problems of weak governance that could threaten the other three pillars of its development agenda. An integral part of Vietnam's transition from low- to middle-income society and beyond will depend on how well it manages the transition from a largely rural to an urban industrial economy — a transition that is now well under way.

However, there are various challenges that need to be addressed seriously in order to avert any negative consequences of urbanisation and to ensure sustainable growth.

Economic development

Vietnam's economic growth and urban population growth are driven by the two independent dominant core-periphery urban systems of Ho Chi Minh City and Hanoi. The two areas are developing differently, with Hanoi moving more rapidly into heavy and high-technology manufacturing over the past 10 years, while Ho Chi Minh City still retains its position as the largest manufacturing region in the country. An understanding of what differentiates the economic competitiveness of these regions would yield different policy options to enable these two important regions to maintain their edge.

Notwithstanding the rise of important urban centres, rural areas are still the major source of livelihood for a large part of Vietnam's population and 93% of its poor. For areas without strong economic potential comparable to large cities, a different set of policy interventions will be needed, depending on the local endowments. Investing in people (education and health) as well as infrastructure (roads) and universal access to basic services will level the playing field and facilitate the fluidity of factor markets. This will enable firms and households to choose the best location for economic activities, thus maximising the efficiency of economic development in Vietnam.

Planning and urban management

Planning and urban management in Vietnam have overemphasised on static design principles instead of facilitating the functions of land and housing markets. In order to ensure that Vietnam's cities continue to play a catalytic role in the country's economy, reforms are necessary in planning processes and agencies. Policy priorities should focus on improving integration and effectiveness of planning agencies, which have moved from utilising static to dynamic plans, and on using sharper tools to better monitor actual real-time changes in the land and housing markets.

Urban mobility

Urban mobility takes top priority in cities and involves the development of road networks and transit systems based on rising urban densities and land use trends that also reflect the location preference and demand of housing and commercial facilities. The central challenge is to ensure that the road and transit systems are in place before there is widespread transition from two wheelers to automobiles as the largest Vietnamese cities are not able to accommodate that total shift to private transport. Investing in knowledge, capacity-building and management is also important. In addition, integrating transport and land use planning and development would constitute an important policy consideration and implementation.

Managing urban land and housing markets

Land and housing markets play a critical role in helping urban economies function efficiently and equitably. Public involvement in land and housing markets would help enhance the efficiency of the market in dealing with positive externalities associated with private development and ensure equitable access to land (and housing) assets. One recommendation is to conduct a more focused analysis on housing in different types of cities. This analysis could serve as a guide in the implementation of strategies to deal with transformations associated with the next phase of urbanisation.

Regional cooperation in solving urbanisation problems in APT countries

Urbanisation process, although posing new challenges to policy-makers and society, will be one of the driving forces to the country's development. To encourage dialogue in urbanisation policy, the Vietnamese government has vouched its support in the development of a learning network, together with the ASEAN Plus Three (APT) countries. For the urban sector, the learning network, despite taking various forms, has its foundation in the APT Urban Forum. The APT Urban Forum opens the participation to a diverse range of stakeholders including the governments of APT countries, donors, non-governmental organisations as well as private-sector stakeholders, which can offer a unique opportunity to share knowledge about challenges of urbanisation, policies and good global practices. The APT Urban Forum will be the primary but not the only channel, through which analytical works on urban development issues will be discussed and exchanged with the larger audience. The forum provides Vietnam an invaluable opportunity and platform to work in various partnerships to strengthen its collective knowledge about urbanisation and to offer its best advice and experience to the APT governments.

Chapter 4

Scrutinising Urbanisation Challenges in the Philippines through the Infrastructure Lens

Adoracion M. NAVARRO*

Managing urban growth requires leaders to plan ahead using national physical plans that safeguard land for utilities and physical infrastructure decades in advance, incorporate transport networks (including strategic seaports, controlled expressways and, if necessary, railway extension to the suburbs) to induce factor mobility, and actively pursue urban renewal following slum clearance. Given this, it appears that Philippine urban development planning and implementation have overly focused on housing and neglected other types of physical infrastructure. Moreover, the urban development plans of local government units are fragmented and lack complementarity. This article traces the roots of this state of affairs, proposes alternative ways of responding to the urbanisation challenges in the Philippines, and discusses how regional cooperation among ASEAN Plus Three countries can help countries like the Philippines respond to urbanisation challenges.

*Adoracion M. Navarro is Senior Research Fellow at the Philippine Institute for Development Studies (PIDS). The author would like to acknowledge the assistance of Keith Detros, research specialist at PIDS.

Analytical framework

A modern articulation of past urban development theories can be found in Scott and Storper's article,[1] which explains that urbanisation process is characterised by the spatial concentration of production activities and clustering and sorting in other human activities. An examination of the historical origins of cities would show how these activities in the cities are condensed or polarised in what can be generalised and known as the "urban land nexus" or interacting sets of land uses (Figure 1). Scott and Storper broadly divide this urban land nexus into three categories: the production space of the city where work and employment are concentrated; the social space of the city as manifested in residential neighbourhoods; and the circulation space of the city as represented by

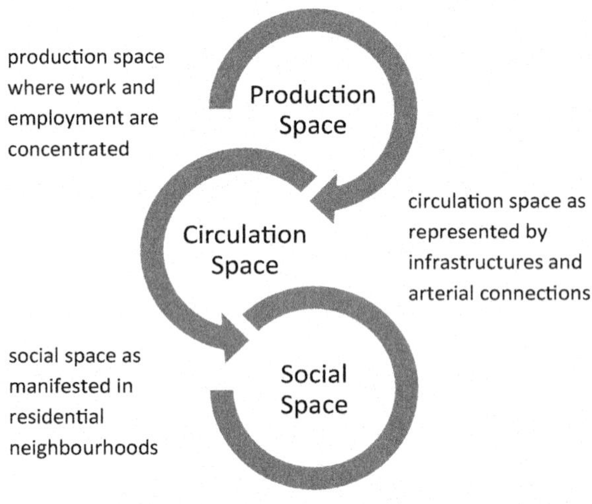

Figure 1. Urban Land Nexus

Source: Author's interpretation of Scott and Storper, 2014; Allen J. Scott and Michael Storper, "The Nature of Cities: The Scope and Limits of Urban Theory", *International Journal of Urban and Regional Research*, vol. 38, no. 4, 2014.

---

[1] Allen J. Scott and Michael Storper, "The Nature of Cities: The Scope and Limits of Urban Theory", *International Journal of Urban and Regional Research*, vol. 38, no. 4, 2014.

the infrastructures and arterial connections that facilitate intra-urban flows of goods, people and information. The circulation space also allows smooth interaction of the production space and social space.

As a corollary to the urban land nexus proposition, Scott and Storper explain that extensive common pool assets and liabilities exist in such nexus. Moreover, in the absence of effective institutions of collective coordination, these common pool assets and liabilities would be subject to numerous kinds of dysfunctionalities such as infrastructure breakdowns, land use conflicts, deteriorating neigbourhoods and environmental pollution.

In anticipating urban growth and urban sprawl, an effective and efficient nexus should incorporate these measures in the plan: allotment of land, build-up of infrastructure, establishment of governing institutions and provision of funds. In the same vein, when addressing urban congestion and proliferation of slums, the urban land nexus proposition should be taken into consideration.

Definitions and urban population trends

In the Philippines, meeting the criteria for the administrative definition of an urban *barangay* (i.e. the smallest administrative division in the country and the Filipino term for "village") determines the level of urbanisation of a town, province or region. A *barangay* can be classified as urban if it meets any of the following three criteria: (a) if its population has grown to 5,000 inhabitants or more; (b) if it has at least one establishment with a minimum of 100 employees; or (c) if it has five or more establishments with 10 to 99 employees and five or more facilities within the two-kilometre radius from the barangay hall. Any barangay which does not satisfy any of these criteria is considered a rural barangay. Under the third criteria, "facilities" could mean any of the following: town/city hall or province capitol; church, chapel or mosque with religious service at least once a month; public plaza, park or cemetery; market place or building where trading activities are carried out at least once a week; public building like school (elementary, high school or college), hospital, puericulture centre, health centre or library; landline telephone system, calling station or cellular phone signal; postal service or public fire-protection service; community waterworks system or public-street sweeper; and seaport that is operational.[2]

As of 2010 nationwide census, the level of urbanisation, or the proportion of urban population to the total population, in the Philippines was 45.3% — i.e. out of the 92.3 million Filipinos in 2010, 41.9 million lived in areas classified as urban (see Table 1 for the population data and Figure 2 for the location of the administrative regions in the Philippine archipelago). The Commission on Population estimated that the country's population had hit 100 million on 27 July 2014 and declared the birth of a Filipino baby at 12.35am as the symbolic 100 millionth-mark.

The National Capital Region or Metro Manila is already 100% urbanised. It is the seat of government and the most populous region and metropolitan area of the country. It is composed of 16 cities (Caloocan, Las Piñas, Makati, Malabon, Mandaluyong, Manila, Marikina, Muntinlupa, Navotas, Parañaque, Pasay, Pasig, Quezon City, San Juan, Taguig and Valenzuela) and one municipality (Pateros). As of 2010 census, its population was 11,855,975 and population density was 19,137 persons per square kilometre. Regions adjacent to Metro Manila have high levels of urbanisation. For example, Region III in the north had 51.6% urban population in 2010 and Region IV-A in the south had 59.7% urban population. In southern Philippines, Region XI, where Metro Davao is located, has a relatively high level of urbanisation, with 59.3% urban population in 2010.

Based on projections by the United Nations (UN), Philippine urbanisation in 2030 and 2050 will be close to the overall rates in the Southeast Asia region (with Southeast Asia defined by the UN as the ASEAN members plus Timor-Leste). The projections for 2030 estimate that 56.3% of the population in the Philippines will be urban and

---

[2] Philippine Statistics Authority, "Urban Barangays in the Philippines", 2013, at <http://web0.psa.gov.ph/content/urban-barangays-philippines-based-2010-cph> (accessed 1 August 2014).

Table 1. Level of Urbanisation in the Philippines, 2010.

	Population	Level of Urbanisation (%)
Philippines	**92,337,852**	**45.3**
National Capital Region	11,855,975	100.0
Cordillera Administrative Region	1,616,867	26.3
I Ilocos	4,748,372	12.7
II Cagayan Valley	3,229,163	11.6
III Central Luzon	10,137,737	51.6
IV-A CALABARZON	12,609,803	59.7
IV-B MIMAROPA	2,744,671	22.3
V Bicol Region	5,420,411	15.3
VI Western Visayas	7,102,438	34.7
VII Central Visayas	6,800,180	43.7
VIII Eastern Visayas	4,101,322	8.7
IX Zamboanga Peninsula	3,407,353	33.9
X Northern Mindanao	4,297,323	41.3
XI Davao Region	4,468,563	59.3
XII SOCCSKSARGEN	4,109,571	46.5
XIII Caraga	2,429,224	27.5
Autonomous Region in Muslim Mindanao	3,256,140	13.7

Notes:

The 2010 total population census includes 2,739 Filipinos in Philippine embassies/consulates and missions abroad as of 1 May 2010.

CALABARZON — Cavite, Laguna, Batangas, Rizal and Quezon provinces.

MIMAROPA — Oriental Mindoro, Occidental Mindoro, Marinduque, Romblon and Palawan provinces.

SOCCKSARGEN — Provinces of South Cotabato, Cotabato, Sultan Kudarat and Sarangani and city of General Santos.

Source: *2013 Philippine Statistical Yearbook*, Philippine Statistics Authority, 2014.

that of Southeast Asia is 55.7%. The projections for 2050 predict that 65.6% of the population in the Philippines will be urban and that of Southeast Asia is 65.9%. Table 2 shows the projections for the ASEAN Plus Three countries and Timor-Leste.

The Philippine Archipelago

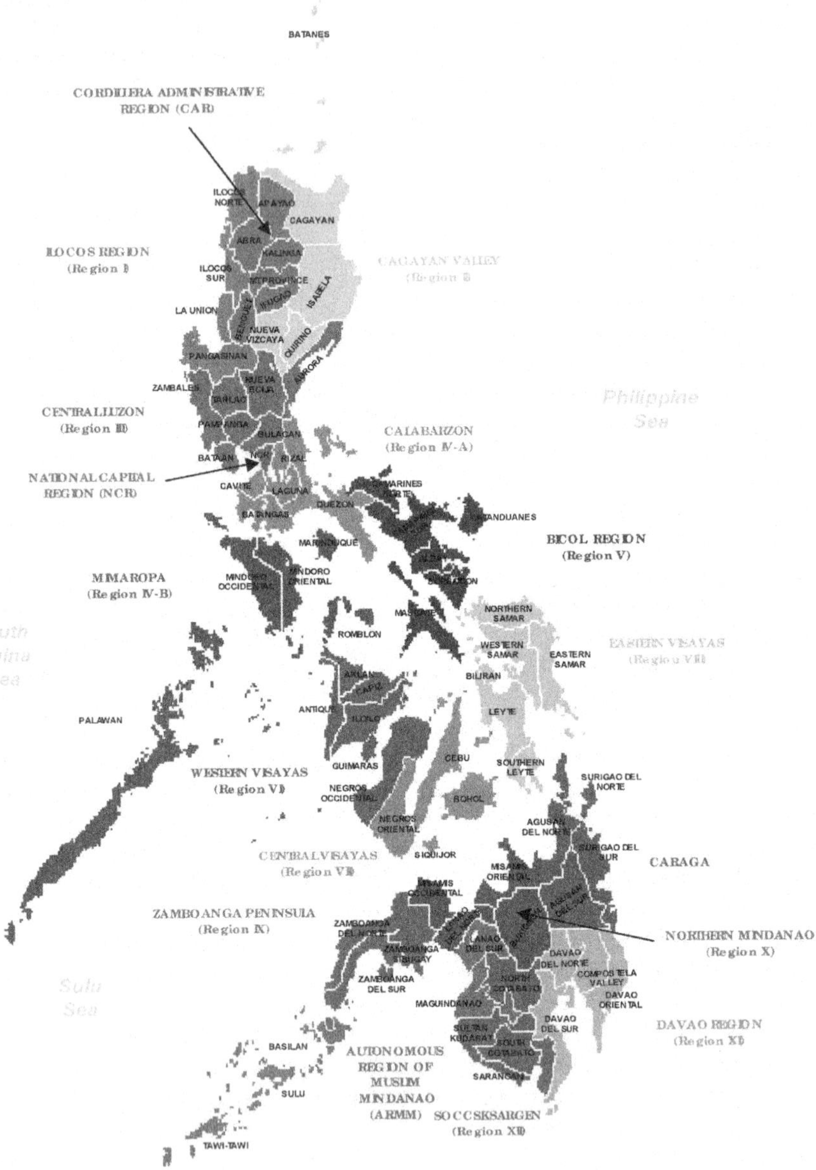

Figure 2. Administrative Regions in the Philippines

Source: E. Villar, 2003, Wikimedia Commons, at <https://commons.wikimedia.org/wiki/User:Seav> (accessed 2 August 2014).

Table 2. Projected Urbanisation Levels in ASEAN Plus Three Countries and Timor-Leste.

	Percentage of Population in Urban Areas		
	2010	**2030**	**2050**
Southeast Asia, overall	44.1	55.7	65.9
Brunei Darussalam	75.6	81.6	85.9
Cambodia	19.8	26.0	37.6
Indonesia	49.9	63.1	72.1
Lao People's Democratic Republic	33.1	51.5	64.6
Malaysia	72	81.1	86
Myanmar	32.1	44.1	56.8
Philippines	48.6	56.3	65.6
Singapore	100.0	100.0	100.0
Thailand	33.7	43.7	55.7
Timor-Leste	28	35.8	44.2
Viet Nam	30.4	43.3	55.9
"Plus Three" Countries			
China	49.2	68.7	77.3
China, Hong Kong SAR	100.0	100.0	100.0
China, Macao SAR	100.0	100.0	100.0
Japan	90.5	96.8	97.6
Republic of Korea	82.9	87.1	89.6

Notes: The 2010 figures for the Philippines are projected values and differ from the actual census data because the official results of Philippine census were not available yet when the UN material was being prepared.

SAR denotes Special Administrative Region.

Source: United Nations, *World Urbanization Prospects: The 2011 Revision*, 2012, at <http://esa.un.org/unup/pdf/FINAL-FINAL_REPORT%20WUP2011_Annextables_01Aug2012_Final.pdf> (accessed 28 August 2014).

Phases of urbanisation in the Philippines

Pre-Spanish growth of settlements and the city-citadel concept during the Spanish occupation

A review of the Philippines' phases of urbanisation can be started from the pre-colonial times characterised by the native settlements. Recent archaeological finds have revised the local and foreign perceptions on the level of literacy and culture of pre-Hispanic settlements in the Philippines. The Laguna Copperplate Inscription, a certificate of debt forgiveness granted by the chief of Tundon (or Tondo in present-day Manila) and by certain authorities in Luzon, revealed well-organised settlements, which were literate, cultured, had forms of government and had pre-existing customary laws in AD 900, many centuries before Ferdinand Magellan's discovery of the islands in 1521.[3] By the time the Spaniards were preparing for the 1571 conquest of Luzon starting with Manila, the thriving community of Manila was estimated to be large — consisting of about 4,000 inhabitants.[4] The rest of the story is a standard narrative of how the *conquistadores* won and subdued the natives of the Philippine islands. The seat of the Spanish colonial government became ensconced within the stone walls of Intramuros, the historic core of the present-day Manila. Meanwhile, economic activities, especially relating to the galleon trade and shipbuilding, sustained the growth of settlements in the Philippine islands[5] and laid the foundations of early urban settlements.

Many Filipino urban-planning practitioners, architects and engineers trace the earliest evidence of urban planning to the time when the

[3] Antoon Postma, "The Laguna Copper-Plate Inscription: Text and Commentary", *Philippine Studies*, vol. 40, no. 2, 1992, pp. 183–203, at <http://www.philippinestudies.net/ojs/index.php/ps/article/view/1033/1018> (accessed 28 August 2014).

[4] J. Mario L. Guariña III, "The First 30 Years of Spanish Rule in the Philippines — Establishing the Legal Framework on Colonization", 2007, at <http://ca.judiciary.gov.ph/index.php?action=mnuactual_contents&ap=j40100> (accessed 28 August 2014).

[5] Antonio de Morga, *Sucesos de las Islas Filipinas*, 1609, translated by J.S. Cummins (Cambridge: Hakluyt Society, 1971).

American colonial government laid out the so-called Burnham Plans for Manila and Baguio in 1905. However, a careful reading of the history points to the fact that even before that, urban planning had long been practised in the Philippines as evidenced in the city-citadel concept, which prominently features the defence plans and layout. This is evident in present-day Intramuros and cities which feature forts (such as Fort Pilar in Zamboanga City and Fort San Pedro in Cebu City). Moreover, old drawings of the plans for Philippine cities have uncovered the Spanish-era planning of space with parallel and perpendicular straight streets for horse-drawn vehicle and foot traffic. The streets cross each other to form a gridiron, with a core square or rectangle forming a central plaza that houses the cathedral and the municipal hall or city hall. In many parts of the country, this type of urban space organisation can still be found.

Urban sprawl began to emerge in Manila in the 1880s and a form of mass transport system to serve areas outside Intramuros was deemed necessary. Thus, in 1882, investments for the Philippines' first urban mass transport system began with the founding of *La Compania de Tranvias de Filipinas*. Between 1885 and 1889, the company constructed a *tranvia* (streetcars or omnibuses) network consisting of five lines, with a central station outside the walls of Intramuros. Four of the tranvia lines were horse-drawn and one line ran on steam.[6]

Urban development during the American occupation

After the 1896–1898 Philippine Revolution that ended the Spanish rule of more than three centuries and the nascent Philippine Republic found itself routed in 1902 by a new coloniser, i.e. the United States, rebuilding and new developments began. In 1905, under the commission of the colonial government of the United States of America, architect Daniel Burnham drew plans for the improvements of the city

---

[6] Gary L. Satre, "The Metro Manila LRT System — A Historical Perspective", *Japan Railway & Transport Review*, 16 June 1998, East Japan Railway Culture Foundation.

of Manila and a new plan for what will be the city of Baguio,[7] although the plan for Baguio was considered tentative due to inadequate surveys. The Burnham Plan for Manila outlined a radial-circumferential road system. The proposal also recommended mixed-use space and explained the functions of tree-lined streets, parks in every district, waterways and waterfront. The idea was developed to ensure that parks, places of work and leisure areas were within walking distance for residents.

Innovations enabled by electricity in the modern world, such as the electric trolley, reached the Philippines when a concession for building electric power and transportation networks in Manila was awarded in 1903 to the Manila Electric Railroad and Light Company (the present-day Meralco). By 1913, nine lines of electric trolleys, which were still called *tranvia* by commuters, were operating.[8] In the 1930s, as the radial-circumferential road network improved, electric- and gasoline-powered bus services were introduced.

However, the implementation of the Burnham Plan in the development and management of urban Manila and the further development of the *tranvia* network were cut short by the war. Manila was the second-most devastated city in the world, next to Warsaw in Poland, when World War II ended in 1945.

Post-World War II reconstruction up to the present

To promote economic recovery, rebuilding had to be done fast after the war, and more so after the Philippines gained independence from the American occupation in 1946. The government's responsibilities in the rebuilding involved roads, sewerage, water supply and security. Housing task was left to the private sector and the government's approach to real estate development was to "let the private sector roam

---

[7] Daniel H. Burnham, "Proposed Improvements for Manila and Plan of Baguio, Philippine Islands", 1905, at <http://www.archive.org/stream/danielhburnhamar02moor/danielhburnhamar02moor_djvu.txt> (accessed 28 August 2014).
[8] Satre, "The Metro Manila LRT System — A Historical Perspective".

freely".[9] The National Urban Planning Commission (NUPC) was created in 1946 to assist in rebuilding Philippine cities destroyed during the war.[10] The NUPC recommended zoning ordinances and drew up city plans, but it turned out to be an ineffective body because its recommendations and regulations could be overturned by the more powerful local governments.[11]

Urban mass transport infrastructure development also stopped as World War II put the *tranvia* out of business. When the war ended, the need to restore electricity in the city became Meralco's more pressing concern and moving people around became the business of ingenuous Filipinos who transformed numerous army jeeps into four- to six-seater jitneys (called *jeepneys* in the Philippines).

Through the years and after the enactment of the Local Government Autonomy Act of 1959, the functions of the NUPC were devolved to local governments and the NUPC played the role of advisor. Inexperience of local leaders in urban development planning and implementation were evident in the rampant growth of informal settlements, residential developments being sold without roads and utilities, "ribbon development" or proliferation of residential and commercial structures along highways and vehicular traffic congestion on the roads.

The practice of not following through the comprehensive urban development plans that were drawn many years before (such as the Burnham Plan) had also taken root, but without the justifiable excuse rendered by war this time round. For instance, the 1941 Harry Frost-Juan Arellano master plan to design Quezon City as the new capital replacing Manila was revived after the war. The plans were revised

---

[9] Alvin A. Camba, "Private-Led Suburbanization: Capital Accumulation and Real Estate Development in Postwar Greater Manila, 1945–1960", *Philippine Social Sciences Review*, vol. 63, no. 2, July–December 2011.

[10] School of Urban and Regional Planning (SURP), at <http://surp.ph/about-surp/history/> (accessed 28 August 2014).

[11] Camba, "Private-Led Suburbanization: Capital Accumulation and Real Estate Development in Postwar Greater Manila, 1945–1960".

twice, in 1949 and 1956, and the government started expropriating and purchasing lands for government offices and public housing. National government offices were also gradually built in Quezon City. However, when dictator Ferdinand Marcos announced that Metro Manila would be the national capital of the country, the Frost-Arellano Plan was deserted. Infrastructure and housing plans were therefore also abandoned, except for a few projects like Quezon City Housing Projects 1 to 8 and other housing schemes for teachers and government employees.[12] Nevertheless, Marcos' consolidation of Manila and 16 other cities and municipalities into one metropolitan region gave birth to the Metro Manila Commission in 1975, which reintroduced the use of strategic urban planning. The Metro Manila Commission came up with a structure plan which defined a framework for Manila's growth through a spatial arrangement of functional areas, land use planning, infrastructure developments and population distribution. Convention and cultural centres, international hotels, the Manila South and North Expressways, and the Light Rail Transit System are products of the structure plan for Manila. However, the implementation of the structure plan was riddled with corruption as funds for public service were channelled to Marcos' cronies who received kickbacks; eventually, many of the projects had to be put on hold.[13]

National government agencies, set up through the years to formulate urban development plans and enforce land use control, zoning regulations and land conversion criteria, had evolved into agencies that did rubber-stamp duties like issuance of permits and licences and less of planning. As the enactment of laws (e.g. the Presidential Decree or PD 933 in 1976, PD 1396 in 1978, and the Urban Development and Housing Act in 1992) and creation of government agencies (e.g. Ministry of Human

[12] Camba, "Private-Led Suburbanization: Capital Accumulation and Real Estate Development in Postwar Greater Manila, 1945–1960".

[13] Marife M. Ballesteros, "Land Use Planning in Metro Manila and the Urban Fringe: Implications on the Land and Real Estate Market", Discussion Paper 2000–20, 2000, Philippine Institute for Development Studies, Manila.

Settlements, Human Settlements Regulatory Commission, Housing and Urban Development Coordinating Council, and Housing and Land Use Regulatory Board) placed emphasis on housing, the thinking and conceptualisation behind mid-term plans and urban development naturally gravitated towards solving the housing problem. While it is perfectly alright to deal with the housing issues, planners should not miss the larger picture that their responsibility is to formulate strategic urban development plans with actual physical targets that take into consideration circulation space, physical infrastructure and connectivity or mobility in the ever-expanding urban areas. Urban planning should therefore involve a closer coordination with public works and infrastructure agencies that have also evolved through the years.

In areas outside of Metro Manila, it is common that mid-term plans are not being followed through, especially when a new mayor or governor wins in the election and discards the former local chief executive's plans. In local governments, planning is narrowly focused on piecemeal zoning and land use conversion. In addition, local governments channelled their efforts largely on issuance of permits and licences when they should have focused on strategic urban planning to materialise the urban land nexus proposition — that is, provide strategic plans to enhance the link within and between production space and social space through the circulation space (including physical infrastructure). According to the law, the Comprehensive Land Use Plan (CLUP) should be drawn up by a local government unit. But the CLUPs of local governments are almost identical to one another in terms of zoning and residential/commercial area development, which are given dominant focus, while plans related to strategic connectivity-enhancing infrastructure are few and unclear, if not entirely missing. In the articulation of CLUPs in geographically adjacent towns, it is also common to find that these plans are not framed by an overarching long-term vision and cohesive strategies for interconnectivity at the higher geographical level (i.e. provincial, regional, island and inter-island levels). Thus, the CLUPs are often seen to be inward-looking, fragmented and lacking in complementarity.

Current challenges and the government's response

Philippine cities are growth centres as incomes in urban areas are 2.3 times that in rural areas, according to estimates in 2009.[14] The Asian Development Bank[15] also reported that urban areas in the Philippines have been accounting for 75% to 80% of the country's gross domestic product (GDP) since 2000, with Metro Manila alone contributing nearly a third of total GDP.[16] Moreover, poverty incidence was the lowest in Metro Manila (2.6% in 2012), the most urbanised city in the Philippines, and to some extent, the regions surrounding Metro Manila. A very large segment of the population, however, live just above the poverty line and are thus extremely vulnerable to slipping back into poverty. Housing problem is also very serious as evidenced by slums and squatter settlements. Traffic congestion and the high cost of moving people and commodities are also very critical problems. Given the archipelagic nature of the country, the proliferation of urban settlements is usually concentrated along the coast, exposing the urban population to climate change-related risks.

In the assessment by the Asian Development Bank,[17] the urban sector's economic growth is seen to be limited by: inadequate infrastructure to attract investment, lack of incentives to promote growth in regional centres, weak capacity for local development planning and implementation, uncoordinated government response, and unpreparedness of local government units for natural disasters and climate

---

[14] Housing and Urban Development Coordinating Council (HUDCC) and Philippine Institute for Development Studies (PIDS), *The National Urban Development and Housing Framework 2009–2016*, 2009.

[15] Asian Development Bank, *Philippines: Urban Sector Assessment, Strategy and Road Map*, 2012.

[16] In 2013, the nominal GDP of the Philippines was US$272.018 billion and nominal GDP per capita was US$2,790.

[17] Asian Development Bank, *Philippines: Urban Sector Assessment, Strategy and Road Map*, 2012.

change. Moreover, there are key problems in economic and environmental infrastructure. These are:

- **Acute shortage of potable water.** It is estimated that less than 50% of the urban population have access to piped water or individual household connections, making waterborne diseases a major public health concern.
- **Inadequate sanitation coverage and poor services.** Communal sewer systems are usually absent in urban areas, storm-water drains are often used for waste-water disposal, there is little or no treatment in existing septage collection systems, and investment on proper waste-water treatment is seldom undertaken.
- **Frequent flooding and rising flood damage.** Flooding is a recurring problem aggravated by uncontrolled building, informal settlements, lack of appropriate building codes and enforcement of regulations, encroachments onto river rights-of-way, indiscriminate dumping of solid waste, sedimentation and the lack of maintenance of watercourses.
- **Poor solid waste disposal.** About two-thirds of existing disposal sites are open dumps and indiscriminate dumping of solid waste onto open areas and watercourses occur.
- **Inefficient urban transport.** In most Philippine towns and cities, road networks are poor. Moreover, traffic control devices, such as traffic signs, signals and road markings, often do not conform to official standards or meet the needs. Mass rail transport system is available only in Metro Manila and there have been no additional lines after the operation of Line 2 in 2003.

The current medium-term framework for addressing urban development challenges is included in the National Urban Development and Housing Framework (NUDHF) 2009–2016. It was formulated in 2009 by the Housing and Urban Development Coordinating Council in partnership with the Philippine Institute for Development Studies. The NUDHF 2009–2016 aims to facilitate economic growth, develop and strengthen local comparative advantages, and significantly improve the quality of life in Philippine urban areas. It formulated recommendations aligned with five elements of the framework, namely:

i. **Urban competitiveness**. This is to be promoted through such strategies as increasing the productivity and efficiency of urban industrial regions, building on existing strengths of manufacturing and producer services, and focusing on export-oriented activities in globally competitive, core export areas (e.g. greater Metro Manila, Cebu and Davao City).

ii. **Poverty reduction.** This is to be achieved by enhancing rural–urban linkages to improve labour mobility and connectivity among rural producers and urban consumers; managing population growth by encouraging smaller families; and implementing livelihood, entrepreneurial and human resource programmes aimed at poverty alleviation.

iii. **Housing affordability and delivery.** This is to be pursued by linking development plans with local economic investment programmes, unlocking land for affordable housing, increasing funding of proven programmes and institutions, and streamlining housing development transaction processes.

iv. **Sustainable communities.** This is to be promoted by using market-based incentives and disincentives to ensure that public amenities support urban land-use objectives, encouraging sustainable planning and green building, and integrating climate change adaptation and disaster risk management into community and regional development.

v. **Performance-oriented governance.** This is to be implemented by providing incentives for local government units to become less dependent on the internal revenue allotment; strengthening their capacity for strategic planning, investment programming, budgeting and implementation; improving vertical coordination; increasing transparency and accountability; supporting public–private partnerships; encouraging performance-based local governance; and supporting metro (interlocal) jurisdictional cooperation.

The NUDHF 2009–2016 explained the infrastructure component but it is a mere listing and description of projects and there is no articulation of purpose-driven and deliberate facilitation of goods and people mobility through strategic transport. It also did not articulate how urban development and growth corridors can be shaped by strategic infrastructure investments.

Increasing urbanisation in the Philippines will involve major adjustments in housing and employment provision, consumption patterns and social interactions. If we are to look at history, there are evidences of urban development planning with a physical infrastructure focus, yet the urban development plans of today, in Metro Manila and other cities, seem to have neglected the infrastructure focus and the need to facilitate the circulation of people within and between the production spaces and social spaces. Aside from urban development frameworks, actual physical plans or master plans that safeguard land for utilities and infrastructure decades in advance, incorporate transport networks (including strategic seaports, controlled expressways and, if necessary, railway extension to the suburbs) to induce factor mobility, and actively pursue urban renewal following slum clearance are needed. However, it appears that at the national level, the Philippines' medium-term urban development plans have been overly focused on housing, and at the local government level, the so-called Comprehensive Land Use Plans have overemphasised land use conversions and zoning and do not have deliberate and operational plans framed by an overarching long-term vision of an interconnected archipelago.

Metro Manila has a transport plan known as the Metro Manila Urban Transportation Integrated Study that aims to decongest the metropolis and become a component of an overall urban development plan. This plan is currently being updated. Another plan known as the Flood Management Plan for Metro Manila and Surrounding Areas was also recently drafted. However, what was deemed missing in the past decades is a master plan that should contain the following key components: a strategic transport infrastructure that efficiently moves people and goods, smart growth and liveability elements in mixed-used plans in compact community developments, enforcement of slum clearance and urban renewal at the local government level, and implementation of flood management strategies that control growth in flood-prone areas. The emphasis in planning should be long term and not medium term that can be easily supplanted after a change in political leadership.

Recently, the Japan International Cooperation Agency (JICA)[18] formulated a "Dream Plan" for Metro Manila and the neighbouring Central Luzon (Region III) and Southern Tagalog (Region IV-A), a big conglomeration of urban areas that JICA calls the Greater Capital Region. The plan up to 2030 will cost US$57 billion and proposes short-term projects aimed to decongest Metro Manila, and medium- to long-term strategic infrastructure projects aimed to enhance connectivity with adjoining regions. The connectivity-enhancing projects include the development of the North-South Commuter Rail system, the construction of the Mega-Manila Subway, the redevelopment of Subic and Batangas ports and control of the expansion of Manila ports, and the development of the Clark Airport and a new airport for Metro Manila to serve as main gateways to the country. There are no clear directions yet on whether the plan will be adopted as the details are still currently being deliberated by government officials.

Possible roles of regional cooperation among ASEAN plus three countries

Given the pattern of urbanisation in the Philippines and the constraints that the country faces in harnessing urban development in order to promote economic growth and higher standard of living, it appears that exchange of best practices and financing opportunities are possible areas for ASEAN Plus Three regional cooperation. Sharing of best practices and financing efforts would be crucial in addressing the emerging physical infrastructure issues in Philippine urban areas. The Philippines also needs to have solid information on alternatives to its

[18] Japan International Cooperation Agency, JICA video presentation of infrastructure roadmap for Mega Manila, released in 2014, at <http://www.jica.go.jp/philippine/english/office/topics/news/140619.html> (accessed 28 August 2014).

current institutional set-up, including incentives designed for planning and implementing government units, and must be able to elicit discussions about best country practices through regional cooperation.

Urbanisation is a major driver of infrastructure investments. Strategic infrastructure investments can also steer the direction of urbanisation, specifically the extent of urban sprawl and the subsequent demand for basic services. The Philippines needs to assess the consequences of urban sprawl and further motorisation, which in turn leads to higher energy consumption and pollution. The knowledge of different country experiences on motorisation and mass transit (e.g. rail or bus rapid transit systems) as an alternative option will be very useful for the Philippines.

The rise in urbanisation requires strategic investments in mass transport, highways, bridges, ports, airports, water distribution networks, electric power systems, and telecommunications and information infrastructure. The Philippines is targeting to spend 5% of GDP annually in these infrastructure sectors but so far it is nowhere near this target as public infrastructure spending as a share of GDP ranged between a low of 1.40% to a high of 2.09% in the 2008–2012 period.[19]

The major constraint to meeting the target in previous years was resource availability. However, today, the Philippines has wider fiscal space, therefore more public resources are being made available for infrastructure investments. The more serious short-term constraints presently are the weak capacity of government agencies to absorb more funds and implement projects. Regional cooperation such as sharing of best practices and innovations in procurement, contractual arrangements, project management and project implementation may help to address and solve the short-term problem on absorptive capacity of government agencies. Partnerships in dynamic capacity-building for government personnel and managers could also be considered. In the longer term, regional cooperation could involve mobilising financial resources to achieve and sustain the target infrastructure investment-GDP ratio.

[19] Adoracion Navarro and Gilberto Llanto, "Financing Infrastructure in the Philippines: Fiscal Landscape and Resources Mobilization", Discussion Paper 2014-01, 2013, Philippine Institute for Development Studies, Manila.

Chapter 5

Managing Malaysia's Urbanisation Challenge

Mazlena MAZLAN*

Malaysia's phases of urbanisation

Early stages of urbanisation

The early stage of Malaysia's urbanisation has its origins in the pre-independence days. The earliest urban towns of Malaysia are made up of port and mining towns of Kuala Lumpur, Klang, Penang, Melaka, Ipoh, Taiping, Seremban and Johor Bahru — a result of British administration and intervention. It is during the British administration that physical planning officially began. In 1801, a Committee of Assessors was set up in Penang, and was subsequently expanded to other states in the country.[1]

Contrary to the conventional sources of urban growth that stems from internal movement of people from the rural areas, initial urban dwellers of Malaya were mainly migrant workers from China, brought

* Mazlena Mazlan was a Researcher with the Economics Unit at the Institute of Strategic and International Studies (ISIS) Malaysia until September 2014. She is currently a columnist at *New Straits Times* in Malaysia.

[1] Federal Department of Town and Country Planning Peninsular Malaysia, *About Us: History of Establishment*, at <http://www.townplan.gov.my/en_content.php?ID=18> (accessed 6 October 2015).

in by the British as mine workers, and from India, who were working as support staff in the Public Works Department. A smaller number of urban residents were British administrators.

During these initial years, the number of local Malays in the urban areas was small, made up of the more educated working in lower-ranking administrative services.[2] In other words, early urbanisation in Malaysia (or Malaya) was such that urban areas were made up of "foreign" towns, with little participation from the local Malays who were still confined to the rural areas, performing traditional economic activities. Rural areas were also separated from the urban towns by distinct administrative boundaries and economic activities, and significantly lower standard of infrastructure and services. Population growth mainly comes from natural growth and international migration.

The period of rapid urbanisation

The usual formation and growth of urban areas resulting from population movement from rural to urban only took place in the 1970s, and even then, it was as a result of deliberate government policies. The divide-and-rule policy from the colonial era in Malaya had resulted in racial segregation, physically and economically. The Malays were in the villages performing traditional economic activities, the Chinese in the cities were engaged in mining and business activities, and the Indians worked in plantation estates as plantation workers. Racial tension flared due to wide income disparities, and reached its peak during the 1969 racial riots. Affirmative action policies which were instituted in the aftermath of the riot sought to restructure the society and economy.

These policies, contained in the New Economic Policy, were a turning point for Malaysia. The New Economic Policy and later the rapid industrialisation in the 1980s and 1990s have opened up opportunities

---

[2] Abdul Samad Hadi, Shaharudin Idrus, Abdul Hadi Harman Shah and Ahmad Fariz Mohamed, "Critical Urbanisation Transitions in Malaysia: The Challenge of Rising Bernam to Linggi Basin Extended Mega Urban Region", *Akademika*, vol. 81, no. 2, 2011, pp. 11–21.

for rural youth to participate in education and economic activities, leading to a large number of them migrating to the urban areas. Also taking place in Malaysia during the late 1960s and early 1970 was the communist insurgencies, to which the Malaysian government responded by undertaking a nationwide compulsory resettlement of the people to subdue the communist influence. This contributed to the rapid growth of urban areas. Malaysia then witnessed the emergence of urban conurbations, new towns and economic corridors. The antithesis of this is the decline of rural population, as well as old towns that are the former mining towns fully exhausted of their resources.

Beginning in the mid-1970s, urban planning became more organised. The Town and Country Planning Act was legislated in 1976 to govern urban planning. Since then, Malaysia's approach to urban planning has switched from a blueprint-based planning to a planning based on development plans, which consist of structural and local plans. The act has been revised four times to keep up with the best practices in town planning. In addition, the government also set up several public agencies to implement development policies in the 1970s. The Urban Development Authority (UDA) was set up in 1971 to develop cities, public housing and commercial centres. Meanwhile, Regional Development Authorities (RDAs) were entrusted with rural development.

Malaysia's urban landscape in the 21st century

In the last 40 years, the landscape of urban Malaysia has been markedly transformed. Malaysia has achieved a high level of urbanisation. From a humble beginning of 26.8% in 1970, Malaysia's urbanisation level in 2010 had reached 70.9%, and is expected to rise further to 75% by 2020. The United Nations estimated that nearly 90% of Malaysians will live in cities by 2050. The states of Penang and Selangor has achieved an urbanisation level of more than 90%, while the federal territories of Kuala Lumpur and Putrajaya are fully urbanised. The number of towns has also rapidly increased, from 72 towns in 1980 to 228 towns in 2010. A major factor that contributed to the rapid growth in the number of towns is the government policy of balanced regional development that sought to disperse economic activities throughout the country by creating regional economic corridors.

With the increasing number of towns and a high level of urbanisation, the pattern of migration is changing. Instead of rural-urban migration, urban-urban and even urban-rural migrations are increasingly common. Urban-urban migration made up about two-thirds of total internal migration between 1995 and 2000, up from about 50% of total internal migration in the 1986–1991 period.[3] Rural-urban migration, on the other hand has fallen from 17% to 12%. In 2011, rural-urban migration had fallen to 6.4%, while urban-urban and urban-rural migration increased to 58.5% and 24.3%, respectively.[4]

The government policies in the 1990s has completely transformed Malaysia's urban landscape with the completion of many significant development projects, such as the new federal administrative capital of Putrajaya, the Kuala Lumpur twin towers, the Light Railway Transit (LRT) system and Kuala Lumpur International Airport. The government has also been relatively successful in eliminating squatter settlements by undertaking a zero-squatter policy, which involves relocating former squatters into public housing. The City Hall had managed to reduce the number of people living in squatter areas in Kuala Lumpur from 134,345 in 1996 to only 15,580 in 2012.[5] The government had spent RM1.73 billion to construct public housing for the former residents of squatter areas in Kuala Lumpur alone. The total number of public housing in Kuala Lumpur had reached 71,031 units in 99 areas in 2012.[6] Transport network has tremendously increased although

[3]Tey Nai Peng, "Internal Migration and Socio-demographic Changes in Malaysia", paper presented at International Conference on "Migration, Urbanisation and Development", jointly organised by National Population and Family Development Board and University of Malaya, 8 July 2013.

[4]Department of Statistics Malaysia, *Migration Survey Report, Malaysia 2011*, 2011.

[5]Ministry of Housing and Local Government (MHLG), *Mesyuarat Majlis Perumahan Negara Bil 1/2006 Kertas Kerja 2,* Putrajaya, MHLG, 2006; and MHLG, *Laporan Perangkaan Tahunan 2012,* Putrajaya, MHLG, 2012.

[6]Syafiee Shuid, 2013, "Case Studies in Public Housing: Kuala Lumpur", in *Housing the Nation: Policies, Issues and Prospects*, Cagamas Holdings Berhad, 2013, pp. 225–238.

congestion and road accidents are still a big concern. There are 19 controlled-access expressways in Klang Valley alone, with six more in the planning stage, many of these are built not only to shorten travel distance and time, but as a response to congestion in existing non-controlled access roads. Public transport has also seen some improvements over the years, although the government is still grappling with performance and connectivity issues, as well as low ridership. An official study showed that the average journey time during peak hours for every working day from suburban areas of the Klang Valley to the Central Business District of Kuala Lumpur is 300 minutes.[7]

Environmental damage, urban poverty and crime have become part and parcel issues of urban Malaysia. Finally, urbanisation is putting pressure on the government to find means to manage its resources — land, water and energy — efficiently, because problems such as skyrocketing land prices that render house prices unaffordable to average urbanites, acute water shortage and rising energy costs begin to emerge as a result of immense demand pressure from the increasing urban population.

Towards building vibrant and liveable cities

The Malaysian government is adamant in ensuring that their cities are not only generators of economic growth, but are also vibrant and liveable. A number of urban management policies have been put in place as the government became aware that managing the inevitable issues that accompany the urbanisation process is becoming increasingly challenging. The Ministry of Housing and Local Government, which is in charge of urban planning and many other related policies, had its name changed to the Ministry of Urban Wellbeing, Housing and Local Government, reflecting that urban well-being has become the government's priority. The ministry has recently set up a Centre of Excellence

---

[7] Nor Fanim Mohd Amin, "Connecting Transportation Networks and Housing", in *Housing the Nation: Policies, Issues and Prospects*, Cagamas Holdings Berhad, 2013, pp. 323–342.

for Urban Wellbeing and Happiness, and this has manifested that the government is serious about adopting the best practices in urban planning. The government has also made a paradigm shift in measuring the country's well-being by switching from the Malaysia Quality of Life Index to the Malaysia Well-being Index.

The country's commitment to urban well-being is also evident in its focus on sustainable urbanisation in the national transformation programmes. One of the 12 National Key Economic Areas (NKEAs) under the Economic Transformation Programme is the Greater Kuala Lumpur/Klang Valley, which aims to transform greater Kuala Lumpur to a liveable and high-income city. This NKEA has several projects in the pipeline, such as the River of Life, which cleans up the badly polluted Klang and Gombak Rivers that flow in the Klang Valley, and transforms the areas near the river banks into a pleasant waterfront of economic value. The project consists of three components: river cleaning, river master-planning and beautification and river development.[8]

Public transport improvement is also one of the relevant National Key Results Areas under the Government Transformation Programme. The government is fully aware that traffic congestion in the Klang Valley is becoming a serious problem, and that public transportation is extremely underutilised at the same time. One of the drawbacks lies in the shortcomings of the public transport system itself, such as limited coverage, low capacity, low reliability and limited connectivity, and low coordination between different modes of transport. The programme therefore seeks to address these weaknesses, beginning first with consolidating all authorities responsible for public transport under one body, the Land Public Transport Commission.

Finally, the government is well aware of the new problems associated with urban housing. In the last century, urban housing problems mainly revolved around adequate supply and accessibility of safe and proper housing. Government housing policies therefore focused on low-cost housing provision with access to basic services and elimination of squatter areas. One of the strategies undertaken is requiring all pri-

[8]World Bank, *Malaysia Economic Monitor: Smart Cities*, November 2011.

vate housing developers to dedicate a specific portion of their housing developments as fix-priced low-cost housing. With no revision in the ceiling price since 1996, rising construction cost has forced developers to undertake cost-cutting strategies, such as building low-cost housing of poor quality, or building these houses in the least desirable locations of their developments, for instance, in areas afflicted with active land movement or poor drainage and thus considered flood-prone. Most of these urban low-cost housing are also high-rise buildings. Segregating low-income housing from the rest of the society has weakened the underlying fundamental of housing provision and that has given rise to new problems. These high-rise low-cost private housing quickly regressed into slums as they are usually poorly managed due to lack of funds, exposed to natural hazards and elements such as floods and landslides and prone to vandalism. Realising that these have affected the well-being of many urban residents, the government has set up a maintenance fund that can be accessed by cash-strapped management bodies of low-cost housing to undertake maintenance works such as repainting and reparation of damages.

The challenges for Malaysia

Despite efforts have been stepped up to address problems associated with rapid urbanisation, some challenges remain, together with newer ones. Some of these outstanding challenges include balancing the powers of different urban authorities, addressing housing issues, crime reduction and mitigation of negative environmental impact. New challenges would entail generating adequate economic growth in the widely dispersed urban Malaysia, managing varying growths between urban and rural Malaysia, reducing urban poverty and creating sustainable cities that offer meaningful and thriving urban living for the citizens.

Urban planning in this country is a multi-tiered affair. It is guided by three overarching policy documents: the five-year development plan currently at its 11th edition, i.e. the 11th Malaysia Plan, the National Urbanisation Policy and the National Physical Plan, which is already in its second edition. In addition, planning and implementation are made at three levels: national, state and local. As these are developed and implemented by different people at different times, priorities and perspectives change, thus creating coordination problems. Political differences also come into play. Klang Valley, for example, is administered by 10 local authorities. The LRT expansion project was stalled for quite some time due to objections from several local authorities, thereby increasing cost considerably and causing inconvenience to people living around the construction areas.

Housing affordability in urban areas has been an ongoing issue that becomes more pronounced in recent years. Excessive liquidity and rising land and construction cost has led to skyrocketing house prices in the last five years. Private housing developers, who have so far been entrusted with the responsibility to provide housing for all levels of society for funding and efficiency optimisation reasons, have been pressuring the government to relieve them from building not only for low-cost housing, but also increasingly affordable housing for the middle income. As a result, the government has been forced to undertake various housing programmes.

Rapid urbanisation has also placed tremendous pressure on the environment and resources. In urban areas where the political race is tight, unsustainable but popular policies of suppressing prices of resources are beginning to fall apart. Klang Valley is currently mired in a water crisis after eight years of free water supply by the state of Selangor to residential properties for the first 20 cubic metres. People are beginning to feel the bite of the crisis as the federal government risks its position in power and starts the necessary but painful withdrawal of subsidies on fuel and energy. It is ironic that Klang Valley, often hit with flash floods, has to implement water rationing at the same time.

These are ongoing challenges, but new challenges have surfaced. The previous policy of balanced regional development has created a large number of smaller and dispersed new towns. In times of challenging economic environment and weak private investments, the new towns need to ensure that there is adequate job creation to attract talents and sustain growth. Although the World Bank is right to some extent in recommending Malaysia to pursue agglomeration instead of dispersal, reversing the path already taken would risk creating dead towns, like the old mining towns in the 1990s after the resources exhausted.

In this context, it is necessary to manage the multi-speed growth between urban and rural areas. Managing urbanisation is more than simply managing the urban conurbations. Urban and rural are in fact two sides of the same coin. In other words, managing urbanisation requires the government to pay attention to the challenges that urbanisation brings to the rural areas. Many rural areas are facing depopulation, which also signals a brain drain at the local level. This in turn leads to rural decline, thus widening the rural-urban gap further. At the same time, with a high urbanisation level, it is imperative to ensure adequate job creation and growth in cities in order to sustain the large urban population. Historically, poverty eradication programmes have focused on the rural areas, but the trend is shifting towards urban poverty because a larger number of the population have now resided in the urban areas. Nonetheless, rural poverty still remains a critical issue as discussed earlier.

Finally, urban authorities must take into account the need to create cities that are conducive to a thriving society, where people not only work, but also live and play in peace and harmony. This can be achieved by ensuring that urban planning take into consideration the connectivity between housing and transport networks which would reduce congestion and commuting time, the environment and social participation. In addition, urban planning encompasses not only physical planning, but also "soft infrastructure" or institutional planning.

East Asia urbanisation strategy?

Malaysia is the second home to millions of migrant workers and their families from other ASEAN Plus Three (APT) countries. Most of them reside in the urban areas and make up an important segment of urban dwellers. However, essential information on migration in this country and even in this region is lacking. Public policies paid too little attention on migrant communities in the urban areas despite their large numbers. This is an area where regional cooperation can be enhanced.

Information and knowledge-sharing on migration patterns, their quality of life, and the ways migration impacts the socio-economic dynamics and the environment would develop better urban planning not only in this country but also in other countries in the region.

As many migrant workers live in substandard living conditions outside of their home countries and are largely neglected by local urban policies, it is therefore in the interest of all APT countries to collectively promote sustainable urbanisation in the region, taking migration into consideration. Furthermore, as urbanisation has substantial impact on food production, natural resources and the environment, it is comprehensible that a country's urbanisation strategy will also have considerable impact on regional food, water and energy security, regional environment and regional security. Is this the opportune time for the conception of an "East Asian Urbanisation Strategy" to address these issues? Can the existing regional architecture such as ASEAN or APT pioneer such initiative? The author leaves this suggestion open for further discussion.

Chapter 6

The Impetus of the New Urbanisation Programme in China

ZHOU Zhihua*

Introduction

In the recent decades, urbanisation has grown in tandem with socio-economic development to become a rising worldwide trend. The West took the lead in establishing new cities in the 19th century, while the East only caught up with this trend after World War II. Particularly many East Asian regions adopted pro-urban policies to boost economic development, significantly stimulating urbanisation rates. At the global level, urbanisation rose from 29.4% in 1950 to 51.6% in 2010. This increase is projected to continue at a growth rate of 64.1% (developing regions) and 85.9% (developed regions) by 2050 respectively.[1]

China witnessed similar urbanisation growth trends. Its double-digit gross domestic product (GDP) growth in the 1990s and 2000s

* ZHOU Zhihua is Visiting Research Fellow at the East Asian Institute, National University of Singapore.

[1] United Nations Population Division, *World Urbanization Prospects: The 2011 Revision*, United Nations Department of Economic and Social Affairs, New York, 2012.

had been characterised by rapid rising urbanisation rate from 17.9% in 1978 to 53.7% in 2013.[2] The Xi administration took a further leap in urbanisation when it introduced the New Urbanisation Programme at the 18th National Congress of the Communist Party of China in November 2012 after assumption of office. The central government followed with the launch of a compendium to guide the New Urbanisation Programme in March 2014. China under the Xi leadership has exhibited stronger-than-ever ambition in the drive for urbanisation and the intention to use it as the economy's main powerhouse in the coming years.

It is against this backdrop that this chapter has been written; it intends to deliver a timely and insightful study on the New Urbanisation Programme, the new leadership's motivation to differentiate urbanisation from the previous development orbit and the implications of this initiative.

The impetus of the new urbanisation programme

China has made remarkable achievements in urbanisation since its open-up policies in 1978. The number of cities increased from 193 in 1978 to 658 in 2010 (Table 1). Urbanisation rate jumped from 17.9% in 1978 to 53.7% in 2013 and the number of urban residents surged from 170 million to 730 million. Table 2 shows the government's heavy commitment to urban infrastructures in the past decade. The World Bank has praised China for its success in urbanisation and for managing crowded living conditions with very few slums and low unemployment.[3] However, China's urbanisation model in the past decades had encountered many problems and did not meet the needs of the new economic conditions of today.

---

[2] Data sources in this chapter are from *China Statistical Yearbook* unless otherwise stated. National Bureau of Statistics China (1985–2012), *China Statistical Yearbook*, Beijing: China Statistics Press.

[3] World Bank, *China's Rapid Urbanization: Benefits, Challenges and Strategies*, World Bank, 2008, <http://www.worldbank.org/en/news/feature/2008/06/19/chinas-rapid-urbanization-benefits-challenges-strategies> accessed 30 May 2014.

Table 1. Comparison of the City Sizes and Numbers in China (1978 and 2010).

	1978	**2010**
City	193	658
Cities with population of over 10 million	0	6
Cities with population between 5 and10 million	2	10
Cities with population of between 3 and 5 million	2	21
Cities with population of between 1 and 3 million	25	103
Cities with population of between 0.5 and 1 million	35	138
Cities with population of less 0.5 million	129	380
Towns	2,173	19,410

Source: *The National New Urbanisation Plan (2014–2020),* The State Council, 16 March 2014, <http://www.gov.cn/xinwen /2014-03/16/content_2639841.htm> accessed 20 May 2014.

Table 2. Development of Urban Infrastructure and Facilities in China (2000 and 2012).

Index	**2000**	**2012**
Coverage of Domestic Water Supply (%)	63.9	97.2
Coverage of Domestic Gas Supply (%)	44.6	93.2
Per Capita Road Area	6.1	14.4
Per Capita Living Space of Construction Floor Areas (m^2)	20.3	32.9
Treatment Rate of Domestic Sewage (%)	34.3	87.3
Per Capita Green Area of Public Places (m^2)	3.7	12.3
Ordinary High Schools	14,473	17,333
Beds in Hospitals	142.6	273.3

Source: *The National New Urbanisation Plan (2014–2020),* The State Council, 16 March 2014, <http://www.gov.cn/xinwen /2014-03/16/content_2639841.htm> accessed 20 May 2014.

Reduced demand and gross domestic product growth

The reduced demand in the world market since the global financial crisis led to a corresponding decline in the ratio of total export to GDP in China from 32.0% in 2008 to 24.9% in 2012. Per capita consumption by urban dwellers is much higher than that of rural residents

(2.4 times in 2012). With a steady employment rate, large inflows of rural residents into the urban areas are expected to expand consumption in dining and recreation, transportation and logistics services, and raise the demand for the construction of housing, schools, hospitals and infrastructures (e.g. water supply, waste treatment and heating). The Chinese government has thus set urbanisation as an engine for sustainable economic growth by promoting domestic consumption and effective investment, changing the growth model into one driven by domestic consumption from one relying on export.

The need for industrial restructures

Generally urbanisation and related industrialisation could improve economy efficiency since labour productivity is considerably higher in non-farm sectors. Table 3 shows that China's agricultural sector employed 34.8% of the total labour force but produced only 10.1% of the country's GDP in 2010. This, together with the rural labour surplus as a result of the massive rural population base and limited arable land in China, is the driver behind the shift of labour to the non-agricultural sector, which normally generates more higher-paid urban jobs, thus increasing income and domestic consumption.

Despite the immense trade surplus garnered in the 2000s, the manufacturing industry in China remains at the low end of the international

Table 3. China's Sector Distributions (%).

Sectors	Indicators	1990	1995	2000	2005	2010
Primary	GDP contribution	27.1	19.9	15.1	12.2	10.1
	Employment share	60.1	52.2	50.0	44.8	34.8
Secondary	GDP contribution	41.3	47.2	45.9	47.7	45.3
	Employment share	21.4	23.0	22.5	23.8	29.5
Tertiary	GDP contribution	31.6	32.9	39.0	40.1	44.6
	Employment share	18.5	24.8	27.5	31.3	35.7

Source: *China Statistical Yearbook 2011*.

division of labour spectrum and derives much of its international competitiveness from its advantages in low production costs. In addition, a serious excess capacity problem is recorded recently in some sectors, e.g. steel, cement, electrolytic aluminum and plate glass. China urgently needs to improve its economic structure and production efficiency to enhance international competitiveness, to lift low-end enterprises out of their low profit quagmire and alleviate the problem of excessive production capacity. Urbanisation is expected to be an efficient means for industrial structures and resource allocations via urban agglomeration effects.

Problems with the previous urbanisation model

First, urbanisation in China focuses more on spatial expansion than the integration of new migrants in the urban areas. From 1996 to 2011 the urban districts saw a tremendous boost in size by 115.7% and in population by 85.2%. In 2012 though over half of the population (52.6%) lived in the urban areas, only around one third (35.3%) of the Chinese were recognised by their registration status as urban citizens. That left around 230 million migrants working and residing in cities but did not have equal access as the urban citizens to public services and social welfare (e.g. education, housing and medical care).

Second, the urbanisation model exhibits imbalanced urban and economic growth across the country and between the rural and urban areas. In 2011 East China represented 9.5% of total land areas, 38.1% of total population but 52.0% of GDP (Table 4). The income gap between rural and urban areas is widening, with the ratio of per capita income in urban areas to that in the rural areas up from 2.2 in 1990 to 3.2 in 2012. The uneven economic development and increasing rural and urban income disparity have resulted in large-scale migration from rural to urban areas and from the west to the east. As a result, urbanisation rate hit 62.2% in the eastern region, 48.5% in central China and 44.8% in West China in 2012. The higher number of people with temporary urban residence permits in East China than that of other regions (Table 4) is indicative of the uneven economic development.

Table 4. Regional Variation in Urban and Economic Development (China, 2011).

	Total	East %	Central %	West %	Northeast %
Total population	1,347,350,000	38.1	26.7	27.0	8.2
*Urban population	661,230,100	44.8	123.7	20.6	10.8
*Population with temporary urban residence permits	76,825,800	64.8	14.1	17.5	3.6
Total land areas (km^2)	9,599,000	9.5	10.7	71.5	8.2
*Urban district area	1,910,939	21.2	14.6	46.9	17.3
*Area of built district	43,603	46.5	20.4	21.1	12.0
*Area of land requisition	1,842	37.5	21.8	24.0	17.8
GDP contribution (billion yuan)	47,288	52.0	20.0	19.2	8.7

Note: *Urban population refers to permanent residents in the urban areas; the figure tallies with the number of permanent residents registered with public security authorities;
*Population with temporary urban residence permits includes people who have lived for more than a year in a place; the figure tallies with the number of temporary residents registered with public security authorities;
*Urban district area refers to total land area (including water area) under the jurisdiction of cities;
*Area of built area refers to large scale developed quarters within city jurisdiction with basic public facilities and utilities;
Sources: *China Statistical Yearbook 2012* and *China Urban Construction Statistical Yearbook 2012*.

Third, urbanisation in China is highly uneven among cities of different tiers and sizes. Cities with population of over one million increased from 34 in 1996 to 127 in 2011. The areas of built districts in cities at prefectural and above levels increased by 95.8% from 2000 to 2010, while that in counties and towns went up by 50.1%.[4] Table 5 shows that the population living in the 333 prefectures or above cities accounted for 29.5% of the total population, 6.7% of the territory and nearly two-thirds of GDP in 2011. First tier cities such as Beijing, Shanghai, Guangzhou and Shenzhen constituted 2.76% of total urban population, 0.34% of the territory and 12.59% of GDP in 2011.

[4] *China City Statistical Yearbook*, Beijing, China Statistics Press, 2011.

Table 5. Shares of Cities at Prefecture or Above Level in China, 2011.

Item	National	Cities at Prefecture or Above Level	%
Area of land (km^2)	9,600,000	643,200	6.7
Population	1,347,350,000	39,807	29.5
Gross regional product (billion yuan)	47,288	29,303	62.0
Invested in fixed assets (billion yuan)	31,146	15,475	49.7
Number of industrial enterprises	325,609	141,798	43.5
Number of higher education institutions	2,409	2,172	90.2
Numbers of beds in hospitals and health centres	5,160,000	2,449,000	47.5

Source: *China Statistical Yearbook 2012.*

Despite the large number of counties and towns (Table 1), such regions not only are too small to have effective agglomeration effects to attract business investment and population, but also generate higher costs in infrastructure construction due to their remote and isolated locations. At the same time, many inland counties and towns are experiencing net outflow of population. This polarised development cannot produce an overall sustainable economy and harmonious society, as over 70% of the Chinese population is still living outside of the cities at prefectural and above levels (Table 5).

Fourth, the ever-expanding urbanisation has led to serious environmental damages and resource abuses. Though the area of built district nationwide increased from 22,439 km^2 in 2000 to 40,058 km^2 in 2010, it is accompanied by land use inefficiency. For example, many cities established various kinds of economic and technological zones to attract foreign investment. "(O)f the 4,210 development zones nationwide, only 1,128 had central or provincial government approval. Cultivated areas accounted for 55% of the enclosed areas. Of the land demarcated for these development zones, only 20% had actually been used".[5] Many large cities have recorded environment degradation (e.g. water shortage, soil contamination and air population). "Less than 1% of the 500 largest cities in China meet the air quality standards recommended by the World Health Organisation, and seven of these cities are ranked among the 10 most polluted cities in the world".[6]

Fifth, large-scale migration to the urban areas has caused social inequality and tension in many cities. In the past urbanisation process, many farmers were evicted from their land to make way for urban expansion and infrastructure constructions. Reportedly, the farmers were often lowly compensated and abused by the local governments during the land expropriation process. Coupled with the lure of better paid jobs in the urban areas, millions (including most of the land-lost farmers) left their hometowns in search of better livelihood in the cities. However without proper training and access to basic public services, most of the migrants could only engage in low-paid jobs and live in informal clusters on the fringe of major cities. This engenders potential environmental, health, safety and crime issues. The difference in customs and dialects has made most migrants outsiders to local communities, giving rise to a dual structure of two segregated communities and to new forms of community tensions.

The problems of the previous urbanisation process had their roots. The mismatch between spatial expansion and urban population increase derived from the dual land and household registration (*hukou*) systems inherited from the socialist regime.[7] The uneven economic and

[5] George Lin, "Reproducing Spaces of Chinese Urbanization: New City-based and Land-centered Urban Transformation. *Urban Studies*", vol. 44, no. 9, 2007, 1827–1855, p. 1848.

[6] Zhang Qingfeng and Robert Crooks, *Toward an Environmentally Sustainable Future: Country Environmental Analysis of China*, Asian Development Bank, 2012, p. xvii, <http://www.adb.org/sites/default/files/pub/2012/toward-environmentally-sustainable-future-prc.pdf> accessed 30 May 2014.

[7] The *hukou* system was introduced in the early 1950s, dividing the country's population into agricultural *hukou* and non-agricultural *hukou*. The key differentiation was the source of a person's grain supply and not economic occupation. Holders of a non-agricultural *hukou* received grain and other goods and services allocated by the

urban development across China and the urban and urban income disparity could be largely ascribed to the policy privileges that went with the establishment of special zones in East China and the pro-urban policies since the early 1980s. The polarised urban development in regions of different tiers and sizes is a result of not only urban agglomeration, but also hierarchical resource allocation system.[8] The economic-prioritised development strategy has led to environmental degradation. Local government's heavy commitment to physical construction and spatial expansion, rather than the habitants and their living environment, has inevitably led to social inequality and tensions.

Central to these factors is the shifting role of the local government and its development strategies in the past two decades. Before the early 1990s, the central government was responsible for regional developments and welfare provisions to its citizens, while local governments, as the regional agencies of the central government, submitted fiscal residuals from regional development to central government or claimed deficits from it. The serial reforms around the 1990s greatly changed the role of local government and its relation with the central government. With the administrative reform, the central government delegated a huge amount of power to local governments for them to take responsibility for their regional developments and citizens' welfare provisions.

---

government. Those holding an agricultural *hukou* were assumed to engage in farming and received no allocated goods or services. The *hukou* system was an effective way of controlling migration towards urban areas. With the economic reform and the abolishment of the food rational system in the early 1980s, *hukou* no longer prohibited physical mobility or restricted migrants' participation in the urban labour market. The debate about *hukou* today largely derives from migrants' access to urban public services, which ties closely to the *hukou* system. In this chapter, urbanite refers to those with urban *hukou* and access to the affiliated urban welfare services.

[8] Municipal governments use administrative quotas or directives for public resource allocations. Higher-tier cities tend to have more resource allocation than lower-tier regions (at county and township levels). As a result, cities normally have better infrastructure and public services, and more investment and job opportunities, attracting more labour inflows.

GDP growth and urban skylines became the key indicators of the achievements of local governments and their officials in their promotion up the hierarchical political system. With land reforms, local governments became the sole legal supplier of urban land under their jurisdiction.[9] According to the fiscal reform in 1994, the central and local governments would share the budgetary revenues at certain ratios, with the local government keeping most of the extra-budgetary revenues. Housing marketisation (the termination of public housing provision in 1998) brought about a boom in the real estate market; the government further fuelled this boom by setting real estate as the pillar industry for economic stimulation to cope with the Asian financial crisis in the late 1990s.

Under such institutional rearrangements, many local governments claimed to be short of fiscal revenues for regional development and welfare provision. They have great incentive to engage in land sales, which are classified as extra-budgetary revenues. The period of 1995–2010 witnessed a real estate investment growth of more than 15 times from 314.90 billion yuan to 4,825.94 billion yuan, and a rise in employment in the construction sector from 14.98 million to 41.60 million. Table 6 shows that local government's fiscal revenues from land sales

---

[9] Before the mid 1980s the government allocated land to users (publicly owned enterprises or agencies) for free. However such free allocation of land use resulted in serious economic inefficiency. This, plus the introduction of privately owned enterprises (including foreign enterprises and joint ventures) by the economic open-up, triggered the land reform separating land-use rights from ownership in the mid 1980s. While urban land is state-owned, rural land is collectively owned by farmers; the use rights of urban land could be leased to private sectors for business uses, but the use right of rural land is strictly prohibited. The government is the only actor that can change the land title-ship from rural to urban use via expropriation and lease the use right of urban land for commercial use in compliance with urban planning. Private actors could obtain the land use rights for certain period from the local government after paying the fee for land use right transfers. Such payment is classified as extra-budgetary revenue and the local government could keep most of it for regional development. Land sale in this chapter refers to the transfer of land use rights.

Table 6. Contribution of Land Sector to Fiscal Income of Local Government (billion, m^2 and %).

Year	Land Revenue	Fiscal Income of Local Government	%
2004	589.4	1,189.3	49.6
2005	550.5	1,510.1	36.6
2006	767.7	1,830.4	41.9
2007	1,300.0	2,356.5	55.2
2008	960.0	2,864.5	33.5
2009	1,591.0	3,258.1	48.8
2010	2,939.4	4,061.3	72.4
2011	3,347.7	5,240.0	63.9
2012	2,888.6	6,107.7	47.3

Source: The Ministry of Finance, 2013, <http://www.mof.gov.cn/zhengwuxinxi/redianzhuanti/quanguocaizhengshouzhiqingkuang/> accessed 20 May 2014.

represented over half of the total in the past years. With rapid increase of fiscal revenues from land sales, local governments invest heavily in infrastructure construction and iconic projects to showcase economic prosperity and a modern urban image. The enhanced land value derived from infrastructure development is captured by more land sales, which further contribute to the construction of more infrastructures. A loop has been seen among land development, fiscal income, urban landscape and regional GDP growth. This is widely known as the *land breeding land* model of urban development[10] pioneered by the entrepreneurial local government.[11] In such land activities, local governments prefer rural land expropriation to the redevelopment of the run-down urban

[10] Ago Yeh, *Dual Land Market and Internal Spatial Structure of Chinese Cities*, in Laurence Ma and Fulong Wu (eds), *Restructuring the Chinese Cities: Changing Society, Economy and Space*, Abingdon, Routledge, 2005, pp. 59–79.

[11] John Friedmann, *China's Urban Transition*, Minneapolis, University of Minnesota Press, 2005.

areas which involves complicated demolition procedures, leading to mass spatial expansion in the past decades. Meanwhile, local governments are reluctant grant land-lost farmer urban *hukou* and related welfare to integrate them into urban society. The over-construction also gave rise to "ghost cities", cities with relatively unoccupied mega malls and skyscrapers.

Strong government involvement in urban development has been observed in China. The premise is that government intervention is necessary to rectify market failure in public resource uses and to safeguard the natural and the built environment. However Overman and Venables rebut that "there is no presumption that an unregulated free market pattern of urban development is socially efficient".[12] The serial reforms around the early 1990s have enabled local governments to play a decisive role in the direction and degree of public investment, infrastructure construction and resource allocations. Local government takes the role of not only a governor, but also an interest-involved player (e.g. land supplier). To achieve high GDP rates and modern urban landscapes, some even play an entrepreneur-like role in the form of shares or affiliations in project developments. Local governments sometimes engage in strategic disobedience when they actively follow central government's guidelines which are beneficial to them but ignoring those which are not. For instance, they had little incentive to restrain land and housing prices and to embark on social housing construction in the 2000s despite strong urges from the central government. The divergence in the mindsets of governments at central and local levels is evident. Many local governments care more about the quantity (massive physical construction and rapid spatial expansion) than the quality of urbanisation (habitants and their living environment). The unsustainable outcome of urbanisation (e.g. environmental degradations and social inequality), together with the international economic conditions and domestic economic restructure, underscores the need for a new form of urbanisation.

---

[12] HG Overman and Anthony Venables, *Cities in the Developing World*, 2005, p. 1, <http://personal.lse.ac.uk/overman/research/difcit12.pdf> accessed 30 May 2014.

The form of the new urbanisation programme

After urbanisation was placed on the top agenda of the new leadership, the central government launched in March 2014 the *National New Urbanisation Plan* 2014–2020 (hereafter the Plan), a strategic, comprehensive and instructional compendium for future urbanisation. The Plan sets out the objectives, baseline, four strategic tasks, reforms in five domains, relevant institutions involved and the implementation path of the Plan (Table 7). The Plan reveals the government's strong intention to differentiate urbanisation from the previous development orbit. It affirms that future urbanisation will take the quality-focused and people-centred form, rather than overrelying on physical construction and spatial expansion as in the past. It clearly states that urbanisation will not be implemented alone, but parallelled with industrialisation and information and agricultural modernisation for a coordinated development.[13] The government will devote more efforts to removing the obstacles that have constrained the previous urbanisation efforts by institutional improvements in five domains, namely, *hukou*, land, fiscal and taxation, housing and environment. More specifically, the Plan numerates the objectives of urbanisation by 2020, which is sub-categorised into 18 assessment indexes with respect to urbanisation rate, basic public service, infrastructure and resource and environment.

The Plan tackles the problems of the previous urbanisation model, e.g. the target of inland counties and towns and promotion of megalopolis development to balance urban and economic growth, the establishment of an assessment system for environment protection and a penalty system for environmental damages and resource abuses.

---

[13] As stated in the Plan, industrialisation, information, urbanisation and agricultural modernisation should be highly integrated in future economic development. Industrialisation could stimulate economic development and is the key pulling factor of urbanisation; agricultural modernisation pushes labour outflows and safeguards urbanisation and industrialisation. Urbanisation provides the platform for industrial development and generates more product demands; information is a symbol of agriculture moderation and an accelerator that effectively facilitates urbanisation and industrialisation developments.

Table 7. The National Urbanisation Plan 2014–2020.

Issue	Indicators
Objective	Sub-categorised into 18 assessment indexes in four areas, including urbanisation rate, basic public service, infrastructure, and resource and environment.
Baseline	Quality-focused and people-centred in the form of megalopolis development.
Four tasks	The four strategic tasks include the gradual transformation of migrant workers to urbanites, the optimisation of urban layouts, enhancement of sustainable spatial carrying capacity, and the integration of rural and urban areas.
Five rearrangements	Institutional rearrangements in aspects of *hukou*, land, fiscal and taxation, housing and environment to eradicate the obstacles that have constrained urbanisation.
Performer	The Plan appoints the executors and responsible parties for the implementation of the Plan: the NDRC will take the lead in organising and supervising the whole Plan; the central government will be mainly responsible for up-level institutional designs and coordinate some significant and cross-border events in the urbanisation process; the related ministries would commit to detailed guidelines in their respective fields; and the local governments to follow the guidelines of the Plan and tailor them to their specific situations in issuing sub-measures for regional implementation.
Approach	The Plan states that action should be taken immediately for issues in which consensuses have been reached (e.g. *hukou* entitlements to qualified migrant workers, renewal of shanty houses, compulsory education for migrants' children and county and town development in inland China); some controversial concerns (e.g. the cost sharing of public service provision for migrant workers, the issue of municipal bonds and the reform of farmstead) will progress in a trial approach before wider implementation.

Source: *The National New Urbanisation Plan (2014–2020),* The State Council, 16 March 2014, <http://www.gov.cn/xinwen /2014-03/16/content_2639841.htm> accessed 20 May 2014.

It also stipulates initiatives to reduce rural and urban disparity (e.g. the free and balanced flows of economic factors between rural and urban areas, the establishment of unified labour and land markets and the provision of more financial services for rural economy development), sustain economic growth (e.g. measures to stimulate domestic consumption and fiscal and taxation reforms), alleviate social tensions (e.g. the increase of compensation standard for land expropriation, the grant of urban *hukou* and related welfare to more migrants) and restructure the political and administrative systems (e.g. the shift in the role of local governments from a dominant position to one of a service type, the adjustment of relation between government and market, and between central and local governments, the improvement of the cadre assessment system to demphasise GDP growth). In this sense, the Plan could be deemed as a holistic development package for urbanisation.

Discussions and implications

Three points are noted in this chapter. First, a causative relation is found in the recent urbanisation process in China where driving forces shape the form of urbanisation and subsequently its outcome (Figure 1). In the previous urbanisation orbit, the institutional (re)arrangements related to urban development (e.g. the decentralisation of administrative power, fiscal sharing system, land reform and housing marketisation) and some features inherited from the socialist regime (e.g. hierarchical resource allocations, cadre evaluation system, the dual-track land and *hukou* systems) have shaped the form of the previous urbanisation orbit (quantity-focused urbanisation led by entrepreneurial local government) and accordingly determined its outcome (economic prosperity, real estate boom, massive physical construction, environmental degradations, etc). The problems of the previous urbanisation orbit, the international trade market and domestic economic restructure are determinants of the form of the New Urbanisation Programme (peopled-centred, quality-focused and market-oriented as assumed in the Plan); its outcome has yet to be known though. The implication of this causality is that, the outcome of future urbanisation

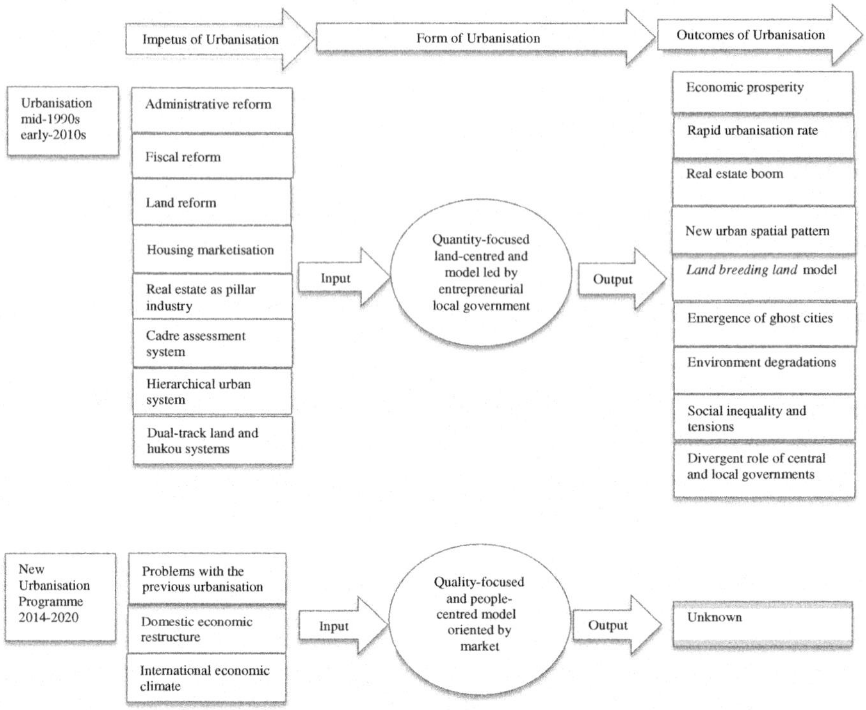

Figure 1. The Causative Relations in the Impetus, Form and Outcomes of Urbanisation in China

Source: Compiled by the author.

is dependent on the peopled-centred and quality-focused form of urbanisation, rather than the urbanisation rate or the number of migrants and buildings constructed. An understanding of how this works will be significant for officials and practitioners who had been keen in pursuing growth rates and building numbers in the previous urbanisation process.

Second, China's urbanisation differs from that in the West. Unlike cities as corporate entities in Europe,[14] stronger government involvement in China's urbanisation has been witnessed, with local governments having a decisive say and an entrepreneurial role in the urbanisation

[14] John Friedmann, *China's Urban Transition*.

process. It also differs in terms of concept. Urbanisation in the West generally is the transformation of land for non-agricultural uses and the concentration of people engaged in non-agricultural activities. It is largely an economic product, though its relevance to society, ecosystem and political concerns is acknowledged. In China, the new wave of urbanisation is mostly targeting at the unsustainable outcomes of the previous urbanisation model, the international economic climate and the domestic economic restructure. The New Urbanisation Programme is set by the government as a holistic strategic package for socio-economic and political development. Urbanisation in China is no longer about the concentration of population and land use transformation, but the coordination of the development of industrialisation, information and agricultural modernisation and the overhaul of the administrative and socio-economic structures. The case of China is unique as it is undergoing the dual transition from an agriculture-based to an industrial economy, and from a planned economy to a market-oriented one. Complicating it further is the dual track in land and *hukou* sectors and urban hierarchical system inherited from the socialist regime. Given the uniqueness and complexity of the Chinese situation, it thus has to find its own model of urbanisation.

Third, no one universal model of urbanisation is applicable to the vast expanse of China though. The analysis of the impetus of the New Urbanisation Programme in this chapter indicates that economic, social, environmental and political factors affect the form of urbanisation, each exerting different weight over time. As these factors are location-specific (e.g. availability of resource and raw materials, environmental conditions and culture variations) and ever changing (GDP rates, policies and social appeal), the urbanisation approach will also be location- and time-specific given the great diversities that prevail across the territory. A city cannot always adopt the same urbanisation path as its socio-economic structure also changes with time. Different approaches are required to match the dynamic situations over time and across regions to achieve sustainable outcomes of urbanisation. Different measures across China should thus be adopted in the implementation of the Plan.

Chapter 7

Urbanisation and Food Security: China's Experience and New Strategy

CUI Haining*

As the world's largest developing country, China's urbanisation has attracted much global attention and interest. As pace of urbanisation accelerates, China also faces many new problems and issues at the same time, among which food security is one of the most important to be addressed urgently. Since early 2014, China has launched a new urbanisation strategy and made every effort to safeguard and achieve food security for a balanced, sustainable and inclusive development of urbanisation.

The relationship between urbanisation and food security

Urbanisation is the historical process by which non-agricultural sectors and rural population aggregate towards cities and towns. Since World War II, urbanisation shows increasingly strong trend globally, especially in developing countries today. However, against the backdrop of rapid urbanisation, food security increasingly becomes an acute issue and is a recurrent topic internationally.

* Dr Cui Haining is Associate Professor at the Institute of Asian Studies, China Foreign Affairs University.

Food security, as defined by the Food and Agriculture Organization, refers to a condition when all people at all times have access to sufficient and safe nutritious food to maintain a healthy and active life. The key question then is what defines the relationship between urbanisation and food security. Urbanisation is considered a double-edged sword. On the one hand, it promotes food security through facilitating large-scale agricultural management but with the possibility of diminishing food-producing capacity through displacement of arable land and migration of rural labour force due to poor planning. On the other hand, food security has substantial influences on urbanisation process. A guaranteed food security contributes to the release of more population and land in rural areas to support the urbanisation. In general, the positive correlation manifested between urbanisation and food security implies that urbanisation and high-quality food security are mutually reinforced and improved.

China's urbanisation and its food security issues

China has undergone urbanisation at an unprecedented rate since 1978 with great success. The rapid rate of urbanisation has at the same time brought about large increase in urban population.

During the 1978–2013 period, China's total urban resident population increased from 170 million to 730 million at an annual rate of 1.02%. At the rate that urbanisation rose from 17.9% to 53.7%, China has basically completed the transformation from an agrarian country to a chiefly industrial and urban society.

More cities and towns have emerged and led the way in China's urbanisation process. During the 1978–2013 period, the number of cities increased from 193 to 658, and that of towns from 2,173 to 20,113. Three regions, namely the Beijing-Tianjin-Hebei, Yangtze River Delta and Pearl River Delta that occupy 2.8% of China's land area, inhabit 18% of total Chinese population and created 36% of total GDP, have become China's main driving force of economic development and platform for international competition and cooperation.

Table 1. Urban Physical Infrastructure in China, 2000–2012.

Urban Physical Infrastructure 2000–2012		
	2000	**2012**
Tap Water (%)	63.9	97.2
Gas Connection (%)	44.6	93.2
Urban Road (m^2/c)	6.1	14.4
Housing Space (m^2/c)	20.3	32.9
Waste Water Treatment (%)	34.3	87.3
Green Space (m^2/c)	3.7	12.3
Middle Schools	14,473	17,333
Hospital Beds (10,000)	142.6	273.3

Note: m^2/c refers to square metre per citizen
Source: National Bureau of Statistics of China, *China Statistical Yearbook 2013*, Beijing, China Statistics Press, 2013.

City infrastructure and public service have improved noticeably. The past decade had witnessed great improvement in urban physical infrastructure such as water, electricity, roads, gas and information network, along with enhanced public services in education, medical care and social security. Furthermore, housing and green spaces have also increased (Table 1).

However, China's urbanisation, characterised by low starting point and rapid rate, faces many severe challenges. These challenges include over-rapid land urbanisation that is faster than urbanisation and "citizenisation" of rural people, inefficient land use, inept land management and administration, sharp increase in urban diseases and the restrictive and unfair system of the *hukou* household registration, etc.

As China's urbanisation adopted a low-quality and relatively unscientific development route, many problems have arisen despite the achievements made over the past three decades. In particular, the impacts of urbanisation on national food security are profound and complex.

Rapid urbanisation has led to the loss and pollution of vast farmland, thereby diminishing China's food-producing capacity to some extent. As a result of massive expansion of China's new cities and towns, China's arable land decreased from 11,254.8 million hectares in 1996 to 10,427.8 million hectares in 2005, and this corresponded to a fall in the average farmland per capita from 0.106 hectares to 0.094 hectares, respectively. By the end of 2011, China's total arable land had plummeted to a record low of 121.7 million hectares, nearly hitting the food security red line of 120 million hectares or only half of the world average at the time. In addition, solid waste and pollution produced by urban residents have also led to deteriorating quality of China's arable land. The Ministry of Environmental Protection and Ministry of Land and Resources of the People's Republic of China reported in 2014 that around 20% of the total arable land was polluted by heavy metals and industrial wastes.

Another consequence of urbanisation process is the shrinking pool of rural labour force. With hundreds of millions of farmers migrating from the countryside to cities for better wages, the proportion of rural labour force declined from 64.85% in 1990 to 43% in 2005. As reported, China's total rural labour force of 394 million in 2011 will be reduced to 119 million by 2025, and this will affect China's agricultural productivity in the long run. However, the condition of the remaining pool of rural labour force does not look optimistic either. The continuous loss of young rural labour force in large number implies that the aged, disabled and women make up most of the rural labour force today. The relegation in the quality of farmers has brought negative effects to China's agricultural production. In some grain-producing areas in China, the phenomenon of land abandonment becomes very serious.

Water scarcity is a serious problem that China has to deal with and urbanisation has further aggravated the water shortage issue, particularly in sustainable agricultural production which is dependent on water resource supply. Rapid urbanisation has resulted in sharp increase in residential water consumption and industrial water usage, thus putting a squeeze on the already-scarce agricultural irrigation water. The share of agricultural water usage was below 70% in 2007 and is estimated to be much lower by 2020 since total water usage will be controlled. At the same time, water pollution produced by cities and towns is another worrying factor that impacts China's food security. In 2011, a large amount of urban sanitary sewage, which accounted for 61.5% of the total waste water discharge, was discharged into rivers and lakes, causing severe pollution to agricultural water usage areas. Water contamination has not only caused a reduction of agricultural output, but also brought harm to human health via food chain.

Last but not the least, urbanisation has dramatically changed Chinese people's dietary structure, which puts new pressure on food production and supply. In fact, the food consumption patterns of rural and urban residents in China are quite different. Rural people's staple foods are mainly grain and vegetables, while urban residents' diet is more diverse, consisting of more animal husbandry products and fruits. However, with the influx of Chinese migrating from rural areas to cities, there is a huge shift in terms of diet and food preference — consumption of fish, meat, fruits and dairy products has increased significantly. As incomes continue to rise, consumption of non-staple food, along with demand for grain, will increase, and this has therefore put heavy pressure on China to produce more food to meet this changing dietary need.

China's countermeasures: The new urbanisation strategy

Since the 18th National Congress of the Communist Party of China (CPC) in 2012, urbanisation has been steadily advanced and accorded with top priority in the long-term national development strategy. Urbanisation, positioned as the new engine for China's economic growth, is not only regarded as an integral part of social transformation, but also a strategic action to address challenges during the transformation process. On 16 March 2014, the Central Committee of the CPC and the State Council unveiled the National New-type Urbanization Plan (2014–2020), which is the first official national plan for urbanisation in China.

Serving as a guideline for China's urbanisation, the plan affirms goals and achievements, draws lessons from the past, and ensures new developments are incorporated with features of inclusiveness, liveability and sustainability. The main objectives of urbanisation as stipulated in the plan are: to improve the quality and level of urbanisation; optimise the urban layouts; adopt a scientific and sustainable development model of cities; and promote a harmonious urban lifestyle and built environment that offers accessibility and convenience of urban amenities. China's urbanisation will embrace the principles of equity, high efficiency and sustainability. In that respect, the plan will execute the new urbanisation process through five dimensions, namely to advance the "citizenisation" of rural population, to optimise the urban layouts, to strengthen cities' capability of sustainable development, to promote the integration of urban and rural development and to improve the process of urbanisation.

In adhering to the people-oriented philosophy, the plan puts emphasis on food security and balanced and complementary development of new urbanisation and agricultural modernisation. The plan recommends the following measures to safeguard food security as China implements the new urbanisation process.

- ***Accelerating agricultural modernisation***. First, China would safeguard national food security and effective supply of key farm products by maintaining the "red line" minimum of 120 million hectares of arable land, improving farmland and water resource facilities, and improving the interests compensation system in major food-producing regions. Second, China would modernise its agriculture by innovating its agricultural technologies and operations, and by implementing preferential policies in land circulation. Third, China would implement plans to facilitate system-building and infrastructure construction to improve circulation and distribution of farm products.
- ***Improving the systems of rural-urban integration***. China has started to establish a unified human resources market to ensure equal

employment opportunities and equitable pay for both rural and urban workers. At the same time, China encourages the formation of a unified market for land under construction to ensure that farmers obtain their fair entitlement of land incremental benefits. Besides, the Chinese government has stepped up efforts to expedite the expansion of urban infrastructures to villages to foster cooperation and sharing of infrastructure resources between rural and urban areas.

- ***Building of New Socialist Countryside***. In the next five years, China will push forward the building of new socialist countryside from three aspects. First, the Chinese government will take a scientific approach to guide the construction of rural buildings and settlements with consultation of villagers' feedback. This will not only protect farmers' production and living, but also keep the rural characteristics. Second, the government places top priority in the construction of rural infrastructures and public service network and in promoting the development and utilisation of clean energy. Third, China will speed up the development of rural social programmes such as enhancing the quality of rural compulsory education, reinforcing rural profession education, improving rural health-care service network and expanding the care and service system for the left-behind children, women and the elderly.

Pathways of regional cooperation in other relevant fields

Although ASEAN Plus Three (APT) countries are relatively diverse in economic development levels, social systems and cultural backgrounds, and also at uneven stages of urbanisation, there exists great potential for cooperation in urbanisation since the countries share key common interests to narrow development gap, and promote inclusive and sustainable growth and the well-being of the populace. Hence, there is plenty of room for improvement in regional cooperation in urbanisation and some approaches should be considered and adopted.

- To establish an all-round cooperation framework that incorporates and promotes market-dominating and government-guiding type of cooperation and public-private partnership to encourage participation of small- and medium-sized enterprises and social groups. The framework is also expected to strengthen institutional exchange and cooperation among APT think-tanks to give strong intellectual support to track-I process.
- To leverage existing mechanisms, such as ASEAN Plus One, APT, East Asia Summit, and trilateral cooperation in initiating urbanisation-related cooperation in the areas of food security and agriculture.
- To identify priority areas for cooperation. Taking into consideration common concerns of urbanisation, APT countries can increase regional cooperation in areas such as construction of farmland water resources facilities, infrastructure construction of highways, railways and air transportation to improve regional connectivity, development and utilisation of new clean energies and extensive adaptation of modern agricultural technologies.

Chapter 8

Urbanisation in Korea: Achievements, Limitations and Transition into a New Phase

KIM Joo-young*

Introduction

Urbanisation is a social process whereby the overall lifestyle of people living in a city changes significantly with geographical and spatial expansion. The relocation from rural area to a city is not simply a geographical movement but a momentum to turn an outdated way of living into a modern one. People have to adjust themselves to the changing ways of living in the process of rapid industrialisation and urbanisation and thus face many urban problems that they have never before experienced in rural area. Korea encounters issues of unbalanced growth, growing gap between the rich and the middle class, poverty and environmental problems caused by urbanisation. Korea has recently made efforts to explore ways to resolve them.

This chapter examines the features, achievements and challenges of urbanisation in Korea, and new developments towards building a vibrant city. The first section chronicles Korea's phases of urbanisation

* Kim Joo-young is a PhD candidate at the Department of Archaeology and Cultural Anthropology in Chonbuk National University.

and highlights the major features. The subsequent sections discuss the past achievements and limitations of Korea's urbanisation process, the challenges it faces today and its various efforts to solve them.

Features of urbanisation in Korea

Korea underwent urbanisation in full swing from the 1960s to the 1990s when the process entered the maturity and saturation phase, and the short span of 30 years had witnessed a shift in the centre of life from rural area to urban area.

Rapid urbanisation occurred from the 1970s to the early 1980s as the migration trend from rural villages to cities accelerated in the 1960s and it can be said that urbanisation is now in the final stage. In 2000, Korea's urban population made up to 88.35% of total population, an increase of 49.2% from 39.15% of total population in 1960. Korea's proportion of urban population peaked in 2005 at 90.12% but has since increased by 1.46% for eight years. The growth trend has slowed since 2005, indicating that urban population has stabilised.[1] This section studies in detail Korea's urbanisation process by periods and the consequent rapid and significant increase in proportion of urban population.

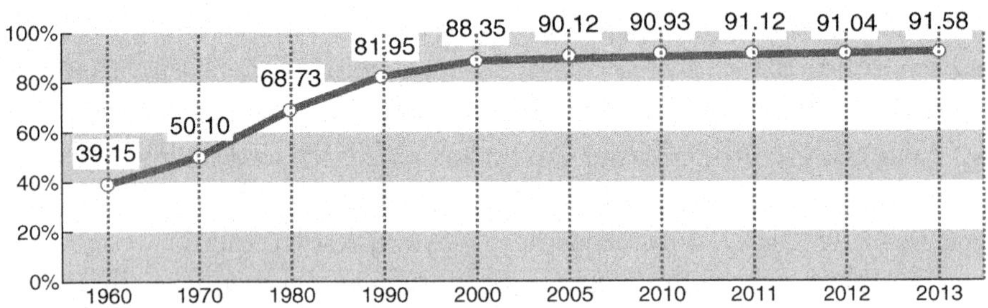

Figure 1. Urban Population Ratio across Korea

Source: Urban Regeneration Information System, at <http://www.city.go.kr> (accessed August 2014).

[1] Urban Regeneration Information System, at <http://www.city.go.kr> (accessed August 2014).

The 1950s

In the 1950s, the population began to be concentrated in cities due to the inflow of people from other countries or from North Korea after Korea's independence.

However, an independent urban planning act was not established yet in Korea at the time and it was still dependent on the Choson Town Planning Act enacted by the Japanese Government-General of Choson in 1934 under the Japanese colonial rule. Cities were planned, albeit inappropriately, in accordance with the outdated act even though Korea underwent rapid social changes after independence.

The Choson Town Planning Act is the first modern urban planning act enacted in Korea and the act was used for mobilising resources including land and population by Japan. In addition, the act focused on establishing cities artificially in areas which were not urbanised for a special purpose, reflecting that the act placed greater importance on establishing new cities and expanding existing cities than improving existing cities.[2]

Korea's urban planning was conducted based on the Choson Town Planning Act until the Urban Planning Act was established in 1962. In the early 1950s, city construction plans were established for Pohang, Gimcheon, Pyungtaek, Wonju, Uijeongbu, Youngdong, Cheonan and Jochiwon from the perspective of restoration after the war. In the early 1960s, rough and ready urbanisation was pursued to respond to rapid population growth in Chungju, Iri and Naju.[3]

With the end of the Korean War in 1953, restoration of damaged facilities was carried out rapidly. From 1953 to 1956, rebuilding efforts were focused on the restoration of infrastructure like road, railway and port, with the support from other countries including the United

---

[2] Yeom Bok-kyu, "How is Seoul Planned?", Salim Knowledge Book 156, 2005, Salim Books Co., Ltd.

[3] Lee Won-bok, "A Study on the Characteristics of Korean Urbanization and the Directions of the Alternatives", Paper for a master's degree at Yonsei University, 2000, p. 14.

States. Therefore, civil engineering work accounted for the largest part of the national land planning.

The 1960s

Urbanisation in Korea began in full swing in the 1960s. On the back of industrialisation policy initiated by the First Economic Development

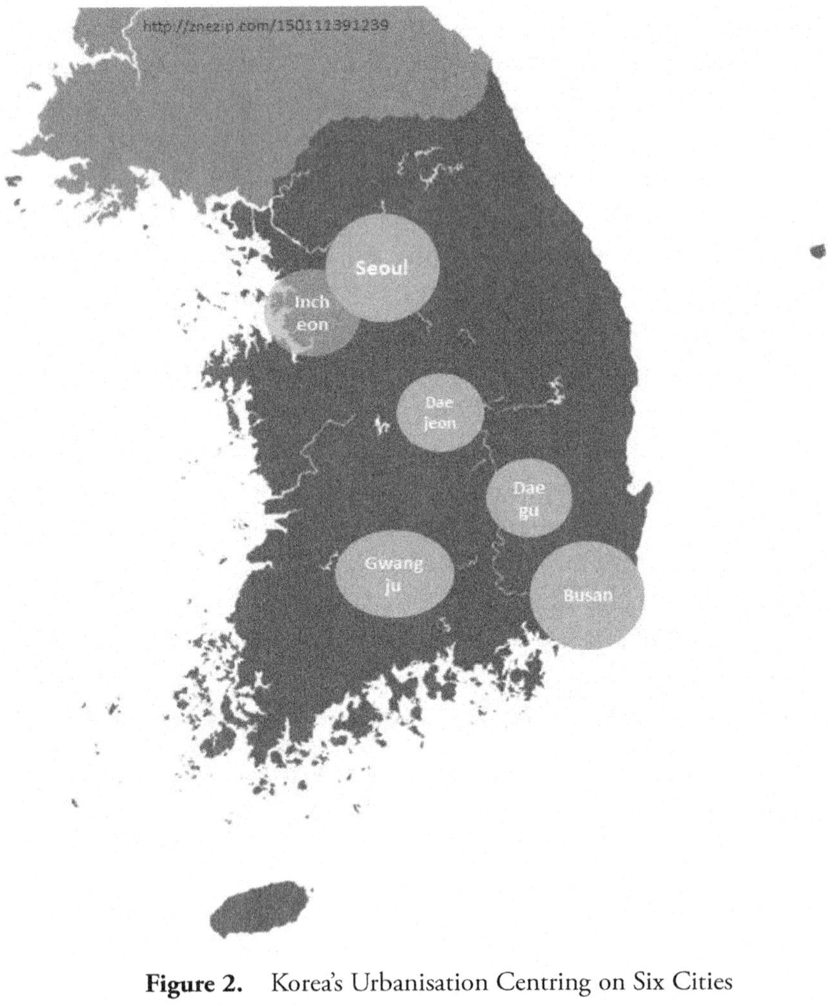

Figure 2. Korea's Urbanisation Centring on Six Cities

Plan in 1961, a massive influx of rural population moved to large cities. Urbanisation was accelerated centring on six large cities of Seoul, Busan, Daegu, Daejeon, Incheon and Gwangju, and the establishment of local industrial complex was in good progress. Population began to concentrate more in large cities with improved mobility of people thanks to the construction of highways. Unbalanced growth started as cities and activities of population began to be distributed along the Seoul-Busan axis in particular with the construction of Seoul-Busan highway.

Korea's urban planning was based on the Urban Planning Act enacted in 1962 instead of the Choson Town Planning Act legislated under the Japanese colonial rule, but the newly legislated act was not significantly different from the Chosun act.[4] Infrastructure construction was mainly focused on housing and road as the existing infrastructure was inadequate to support the increasing urban population. However, a long-term master national development plan was lacking even though there was an economic plan during that period. Hence, urban planning faced limitations in allocating state land efficiently and harmoniously to accommodate rapidly expanding economy and social changes.[5]

The 1960s witnessed rapid changes in rural area along with urban problems. Urbanisation in the 1960s, as a result of unilateral population movement from rural to urban areas, had caused impoverishment in rural regions, public dissatisfaction about the weakened power of the surrounding rural regions, and vulnerability of the rural leadership, politics and national policies leading to social changes as well as conflicts of social structure in rural areas.[6]

---

[4] Lee Tae-yul, "Traces of Urban Planning Acts", *Urban Affairs*, vol. 17, no. 11, 1982, pp. 66–79, esp. 71. The difference between Choson Town Planning Act and Urban Planning Act lies in the rules on construction, which became separate and independent as Construction Act with the enactment of Urban Planning Act.

[5] Lee Won-bok, "A Study on the Characteristics of Korean Urbanization and the Directions of the Alternatives".

[6] Park Soo-young and Kwon Won-ki, "Historical Overview of Urbanization in Korea", *Kyung Hee Law Journal*, no. 27, 1992, pp. 147–173, esp. 154.

The 1970s

In the 1970s, the First Comprehensive National Land Plan (1972–1981) was implemented in response to rapid urbanisation since the 1960s. Under the plan, efforts were made to alleviate population concentration in large cities by developing provincial growth bases, establishing new cities, installing regional branch school of universities located in Seoul and expanding medical system to regional areas.

During this period, the development restricted zone policy was executed. This policy was introduced to designate areas where urban development should be restricted in order to ensure a conducive living environment for citizens, with guidelines to prevent reckless expansion of cities, and preserve the natural environment near cities and areas zoned as development restricted area for security reason. The ministers of the Ministry of National Defense and Ministry of Land, Infrastructure and Transport determined and made decisions on the restricted areas under province, city and county management plan.[7]

The Urban Planning Act was totally revised in 1971 and this reflected rapid changes in Korean society and economy. Revisions were made to address the urban problems, such as reckless development, disorderly expansion of urban suburbs, lack of housing and traffic congestion, which had arisen because the cities experienced rapid population growth that paralysed the basic functions of cities as a result of the successful implementation of the five-year economic plan.[8] The purpose of the revisions made to the Urban Planning Act is to promote development in an orderly manner and establish more rational land use control measures.[9]

Population movement from rural to urban areas had defined the main trend in the 1970s and as a result, about half of the Korean

---

[7] Article 38.1, Act on Planning and Use of National Territory; and Article 3.1, Act on Special Measures for Designation and Management of Development-Restricted Area.

[8] The five-year economic plan for the development of national economy between 1962 and 1981.

[9] Lee Tae-yul, "Traces of Urban Planning Acts", *Urban Affairs*, vol. 17, no. 11, 1982, pp. 66–79, esp. 72.

population lived in cities. In addition, industrialisation had enabled urban cities to be self-sufficient, and thus attracted and absorbed large inflow of population. During this period, the emergence of production theory that emphasises distribution of work, rationalism, industrial productivity as well as collective relationships among people had brought about changes in people's mindset and their life values and norms.[10]

The 1980s

The Second Comprehensive National Land Plan (1982–1991), launched in the 1980s, aimed to settle the population in regional areas, improve national welfare and preserve natural environment. However, the agglomeration of new industries in large cities and concentration of traditional industries in regional areas had caused a widening gap between metropolitan areas and other regional areas. Around the period of the 1988 Seoul Olympics and 1986 Asian Games, Korea also carried out extensive renewal activities, which led to destruction of residences of the urban poor and illegal residential areas.

In the 1980s, Korea's urbanisation was characterised by suburbanisation — that is, the birth of new satellite cities in Gyeonggi-do near Seoul.[11] Satellite cities grew in the vicinity of large cities due to population movement to suburban areas where economic activities were located, and this situation was witnessed in most cities after the 1980s. Despite the positive effects generated from construction of new cities such as stable housing prices and increased housing supply, there is criticism that the policy caused concentration of population in metropolitan areas as well as reckless development. In addition, new cities in the early days fell into the bed-town trend because these cities, due to

---

[10] Park Soo-young and Kwon Won-ki, "Historical Overview of Urbanization in Korea", pp. 147–173, esp. 155.

[11] Moon Suk-nam, "Urbanization in Korea: Its Pattern and Characteristics", *Regional Development Research*, vol. 29, 1996, pp. 29–66, esp. 43.

the lack of economic self-sufficiency, failed to achieve the job-housing proximity target.[12]

Urbanisation accelerated in the late 1980s and this can be attributed to the promotion of heavy and chemical industries and export industry in the 1970s, which had contributed to the establishment of production and employment structures, labour market, and consumption and distribution structures, thus producing new jobs and opportunities to generate income in the cities.[13] In particular, the 1980s had witnessed significant development in transportation and communications that catalysed the formation of metropolitan city area.

The 1990s

The Third Comprehensive National Land Plan (1992–2001), announced in the 1990s, focused on population reduction in the metropolitan area and areas located alongside the Seoul-Busan line and aimed to establish a decentralised national land structure. Apparently, large cities with population of more than one million have shown signs of stagnant growth while small- and medium-sized cities with population between 0.2 million to one million have continued to grow.

Urban population growth after 1990 seemed to be led by mid-sized cities of population size between 0.2 million to one million but those cities were mostly located in the metropolitan areas. Gyeonggi-do, in particular, witnessed rapid population movement due to construction of new cities in the 1980s. This in turn led to population concentration in metropolitan areas once again and stagnation in population growth in non-metropolitan areas, and as a result, unbalanced development between metropolitan area and non-metropolitan area became a new

[12] Lee Soo-hang, Moon Mi-sung, Jang Yoon-bae, Park In-seong, Chae Myoung-jin and Choi Seong-woong, "A Comparative Study on the Urbanization Process between Korea and China", Gyeonggi Research Institute, 2011, p. 29.

[13] Cho Myung-rae, "Reflections on Korean Cities: Trend and Prospect of Urbanization in Korea", *Economy and Society*, vol. 60, 2003, pp. 10–39, esp. 22.

national agenda.[14] The trend continued in the 2000s but with greater emphasis on balanced development and decentralisation.

Achievements and challenges of urbanisation in Korea

Achievements

That economic development promoted urbanisation is one of the underlying characteristics of urbanisation in Korea has been corroborated by the remarkable growth largely achieved by the six large cities of Seoul, Busan, Daegu, Daejeon, Incheon and Gwangju — the key bases for industrialisation. Korea's spectacular economic development, which was achieved within 50 years, is aptly called the "Miracle on the Han River".

Indeed, rapid economic growth has yielded material affluence. Korea's gross national income (GNI) per capita was US$79 in 1962 and export volume was US$55 million. The Korean government launched its economic development plan in the 1960s to expand economic scale and achieve growth. Korea subsequently witnessed rapid economic growth.[15] As of 2013, its gross domestic product ranked 15th at US$1.1975 trillion and its per capita GDP ranked at 33rd in the world at US$23,837.[16]

Urbanisation in Korea proceeded in tandem with the implementation of economic development plans in the 1960s for the purpose of achieving economic growth. The 1970s witnessed more systematic and comprehensive national land planning. In the 1980s, as the gap between metropolitan area and other regions began to widen, the

[14] Cho Myung-rae, "Urbanization in Korea and the Fate of Region", *Hwang Hae Review*, 2010, pp. 32–53, esp. 47.

[15] Lee Soo-hang, Moon Mi-sung, Jang Yoon-bae, Park In-seong, Chae Myoung-jin and Choi Seong-woong, "A Comparative Study on the Urbanization Process between Korea and China", p. 26.

[16] International Monetary Fund.

government introduced strategies to distribute growth and solve the problems of unbalanced development by redistributing industrial complexes to other regions and developing regional communities. Impressive achievements were made during this period in terms of improved living environment for people, resource development, expansion in national land development and redesign of spatial structure.

In the 1990s, extensive efforts were made to form decentralised national land structure to resolve the issues of unbalanced national development and make national land acquisition competitive amid globalisation and regionalism. In particular, the application and upgrading of science and technology in response to challenges of globalisation had proven to be effective.[17]

Challenges

Despite the material affluence that urbanisation has generated, not everyone has enjoyed the fruits of urbanisation. A series of historical events including independence, division of Korea and Korean War resulted in social changes, which were however not addressed properly as the Korean government pursued and implemented urbanisation in tandem with industrialisation. In addition, the authority had not taken into consideration specific conditions of each city in implementing urbanisation, which was promoted as a part of industrialisation at the national level.

The national land development during the period when urbanisation progressed in full force focused on large-scale civil engineering and construction works like building of industrial complexes and construction of highways and ports, thus resulting in a lack of supporting infrastructure that cater to urban citizens.

Housing redevelopment was part of the urban improvement that the authority focused on as it is relatively profitable and easy to reach

[17] Suh Soon-tak, "Achievements and Challenges of National Territorial of Policies in Korea", *Public Land Law Review*, 2009.

consensus among stakeholders. For that reason, there was a lack of redevelopment in cities that are business-driven.

It is noteworthy that while urban development projects were supposed to solve the urban problems, these were driven by housing development that primarily focused on renewal after eviction. This had deprived the urban poor of residential rights.

From the late 1980s to 1990s, housing supply in cities expanded, and redevelopment and reconstruction of old apartments became a popular tactic to increase individual's asset. As redevelopment and reconstruction projects yielded huge profits for developers, prices of these old apartments pending for redevelopment and reconstruction soared, therefore causing widespread speculation.

Eviction and renewal had led to the collapse of mutually complementary community, which was built on self-sustainable and various socio-economic opportunities and relationship.[18] As urban lifestyle rapidly transitioned from group oriented to individual oriented, urban citizens have lost the opportunity of communal living and exchange, and of forming human relationship behind the glossy façade of the city.

Challenges like the hollowing-out phenomenon and declining old cities have arisen because cities that are driven by the conventional manufacturing industry have experienced slow growth with major changes to the industrial structure. As the industrial structure shifted from one that was manufacturing based to knowledge-intensive based focusing on value-add and sophisticated industry, it is therefore expected for cities driven by manufacturing to decline. Older sections of cities do not have adequate supporting facilities, including parking lots, parks, cultural and welfare facilities and infrastructure like public transportation network, and many of the aged housings also require upgrading.

Haphazard urban-suburb development and relocation of city functions to suburban area have further exacerbated the decline of cities and

---

[18] Kim Yong-woong, "Paradigm Changes in Urban Regeneration Policy and Tasks", *Planning and Policy*, 2008, p. 149.

their functions. This corresponds with a growing number of cities being discarded as commercial districts of cities decline and population move to suburban areas, which witness the formation of new cities that focus on residential development. It is common in most cities in Korea that has not taken into consideration of the city population size.[19]

Recently, the emergence of new urban environment with population decrease is recognised as a problem. Korea's fertility rate is among the lowest in the world. According to the World Factbook by Central Intelligence Agency of the United States, Korea's total fertility rate was merely 1.25 in 2014, putting Korea at 219th position among 224 countries reviewed.[20] Decreasing fertility rate and growing proportion of population aged 65 and over have emerged as social issues. The ratio of the elderly population was 3.1% in 1970 and increased to 11% in 2010. In this respect, population ageing would accelerate if low fertility rate persists.[21]

Urban planning, if implemented properly, could help adjust the supply and demand of facilities based on demographic changes and population needs including the elderly and multicultural families.

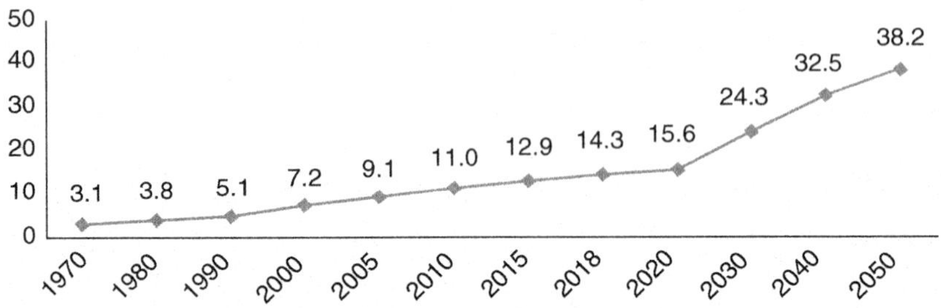

Figure 3. Korea's Growth Trend of Ratio of Population Aged 65 and Above (unit: %)
Source: Statistics Korea, *Future Population Estimate.*

[19] Kim Kwang-joong, "Causes and Consequences of Urban Decline in Korean Cities", *Korean Society for Urban Geology*, vol. 13, no. 2, 2010, pp. 43–58, esp. 46.
[20] "Korea's Fertility Rate among the Lowest in the World", 30 June 2014, *Chungcheong Daily*.
[21] Statistics Korea, *Future Population Estimate*.

With rising number of elderly population, the provision of convenient facilities and welfare policies for them has become a social issue in Korea. The dire lack of facilities in cities for the elderly population has apparently become a tacky issue because the old folks, having toiled hard for Korea's economic development in their younger days, find that they do not feel belonged in the cities after their retirement, other than the parks. The busy city districts have in fact become a place chiefly for the younger generation.

Korea's outdated infrastructure, constructed since the advent of urbanisation 50 years ago, has also posed increasing risks to the safety of citizens. There has been an increase in the incidents of sinkholes and sudden ground collapse recently. The causes of sinkhole incidents, which could be attributable to construction of buildings, waterworks and sewage treatment, require accurate diagnosis.

New developments

Urban policies

In pursuit of rapid growth, the major issue was creating space and facilities necessary for urban living in the shortest time possible. To this end, the government considered injecting large amount of capital investment to build cities was a rational and efficient decision.[22] This was regarded to be a necessary move to plan and construct urban infrastructure within a short time in order to facilitate fast connectivity between rural areas and cities. Korea's high-speed urbanisation achieved in the past 30 years reflected its "can do" and "work fast" attitude, and the emphasis on speed.

Even though growth in quantitative term was achieved, there were questions raised over the quality of growth. Recently, Korea had committed efforts to establish an institution that ensures harmonious integration of development with natural environment in order to curb

[22] Urban Regeneration Information System, at <http://www.city.go.kr> (accessed August 2014).

haphazard development. A policy was also put in place to establish a buffer urban space to mitigate the extent of destruction to cities caused by climate change and natural disasters as well as to address the environmental damage in cities due to land use.

The Korean government had also made efforts in related areas such as conducting disaster vulnerability analysis, designating mandatory disaster prevention zone, decentralising the rainfall management system and establishing an integrated hub for urban disaster prevention.[23] That said, Korea attempts to make a paradigm change in urban policy that involves adopting a gradual urban growth approach, preparing for unexpected risks and pursuing better-quality growth.

Urban regeneration: Rebuilding human bonds and city

Korea has achieved urbanisation in macroscopic industrial process at the central government level. Korea needs to move from the centralised approach and adopt a decentralised approach of urban development, focusing on human-oriented urban regeneration — a departure from the previous practice of eviction and renewal. This is because urbanisation does not simply involve geographical and spatial changes, and the process in fact encompasses people to make adjustments to their overall lifestyle along with changing mindset and values. Recently, Korea launched the "Reviving Cities" projects which emphasise the significance of living and life values of urbanites.

Korea implemented its urban regeneration in the 2000s to revive the economy, society and physical hardware of existing cities that have become relatively outdated due to changes in industrial structure and urban expansion of new cities and new city centres.[24] Under the 2013 Special Act on the Promotion and Support of Urban Regeneration, the policy has made a direction change in the approach — from the private sector-led eviction and renewal approach adopted for the past

---

[23] Ministry of Land, Infrastructure and Transport, "2013 Manual for Urban Task".

[24] Jeonju Test Bed Korea Urban Renaissance Center, at <http://jeonju.kourc.or.kr> (accessed July 2014).

40 years[25] to urban regeneration that focuses on improving the overall urban functions and re-energising local economy. Hence, with this policy shift, small-scale urban regeneration projects that focus on environmental, economic and livelihood regeneration are viewed more favourably than large-scale projects like new town development.[26]

The urban regeneration projects embody two concepts. The first concept, known as neighbourhood regeneration, involves improvement of residential environment and revival of declining commercial district led by residents, and the second concept, known as economy-based regeneration, involves restoration of the urban economic base. Economy-based regeneration aims to cover various areas such as redeveloping ageing ports, developing areas near transportation hubs, public administration and relocation of plant sites, creating employment to capitalise on the city's industry, culture and history, and expanding urban functions that are currently lacking.[27]

This move had digressed from the past approach in that urban regeneration is carried out in consideration of the characteristics of each city. In addition, cities in Korea are trying to find their own unique historical and cultural resources as local culture is considered valuable assets in urban regeneration projects.

"Making a Village" project, which is conducted as a part of urban regeneration projects, focuses on the restoration of relationships in local communities. The objective is to help people overcome problems of loneliness and sense of alienation in their fragmented lives in a city through reorganisation of networks. "Making a Village" project involves reorganising the community that became scattered in the process of rapid urbanisation. At the same time, the project aims to be

---

[25] This is not a criticism directed at the eviction and renewal approach itself. Rather, the one-dimensional urban renewal without considering the city's physical, social and economic conditions is subject to criticism.

[26] Kwon Dae-jung, "Direction of Urban Regeneration under Park Geun-hye Government", *Korea Economic Magazine*.

[27] "5 Economy-based Urban Regeneration Projects Conducted Every Year, 'Key' to Success is Participation of Private Sector", *Aju Business Daily*, 15 July 2014.

more people-oriented and puts people's lives at the centre of urban planning.

For example, Seoul has designated various areas for the "Making a Village" project since 2012. Under the project, places where people hold shared memories are identified and various programmes are also organised to encourage relationship-building based on common cultural experiences.

It would be ideal, of course, to make a village that is led by residents and not by owners. Therefore, the project, conducted through public-private cooperation, values residents' participation most. However, caution should be exercised in taking this approach because in some cases, residents cannot afford to live in the same place anymore due to rising land prices as a result of the implementation of this project after budget allocation. Instead of focusing on short-term achievements, the project should take a long-term and broader perspective.

It is evident from the recent trends that the project not only focuses on physical environment improvement but also on restoring lost human relations and reorganising networks by establishing the community that people need.

Green city[28]

Korea advocates a low-carbon lifestyle through urban greening and energy conservation. The use of energy-saving construction material and creating green space and environment — i.e. by planting trees in built-up areas to reduce or absorb carbon dioxide emissions — are part of this recent trend. New and renewable energy facilities that use sunlight, solar heat and biomass have found expanded applications in commercial buildings and housings. A broad range of incentives are provided to buildings or urban development projects of designated scale that have obtained the eco-friendly building certificate.

It is noteworthy that carbon emissions reduction can be enforced at the urban planning phase through energy conservation and utilisation

[28] Ministry of Land, Infrastructure and Transport, "2013 Manual for Urban Task".

of new and renewable energy. It is cost-viable to build an eco-friendly building or complex, and install new and renewable energy facilities based on the recognition of necessity. Efforts to preserve the ecosystem of streams, establish rainfall management system and improve natural bank to prevent flooding are part of the green city policies. Expansion of parks in a city and development of recreational areas in a city are being planned from the long-term perspective to meet the demands of citizens for improved living environment.

Changing the mindset of achieving rapid growth is required, considering that clean environment is essential for sustainable urban development.

Future research cooperation for a healthier city

An important lesson that Korea could learn from its past urbanisation process is to take into consideration the characteristics of each region at master-planning stage. Urbanisation problems faced by most countries may appear to be universal, but there are distinctions due to the country's unique political, economic, social and cultural contexts. That said, in order to create a healthier living environment for cities, it is critical to identify urban problems in the regional context and then find relevant solutions.

In addition, a holistic approach that identifies existing economic, social and cultural resources of the region is imperative in order to achieve balanced urban growth and this requires continuous research cooperation. The fundamental of research cooperation should be premised on a long-term commitment to solve urban problems by building a strong network of experts and identifying research subjects related to urbanisation. Cooperative research would primarily enhance the understanding of urbanisation and serve as a problem-solving platform to recognise problems faced by each city and dispense appropriate solutions.

Chapter 9

Japan's Urbanisation Experience

Kaoru ISHIKAWA*

Urbanisation in Japan

Settlement in the early era

The Japanese experience in settlement was not unique; it started from very humble beginnings. Early dwellers in Japan survived on fishing, hunting, agriculture (bean, burdock, gourd, etc.) and chestnut cultivation, as well as lived together within a wall-protected compound for security reasons. Archeological sites of these settlements are found mostly in the northern part of Japan, such as Sannai-Maruyama Iseki (with a surface area of 380,000 square metres) where people lived from around 4,000 to 5,500 years ago. Archeological research revealed that they not only cultivated crops but also traded with other regions in Japan, extending from today's Niigata 600km to the south and Hokkaido to the north. This period is known in Japan as the 'Johmon era'.

*Kaoru ISHIKAWA is Director of educational institution Kawamura Gakuen and specially appointed Professor of Kawamura Gakuen Women's University, and Visiting Professor of Akita International University. He was former Director General of Economic Affairs Bureau of Japanese Ministry of Foreign Affairs and former Ambassador to Egypt and Canada.

After the long Johmon era, people from the south migrated to Japan and brought rice cultivation, marking the start of the 'Yayoi era'. Rice cultivation in a mountainous archipelago that was often hit by typhoons shaped community characteristics of Japanese settlement. From experience, the dwellers knew empirically that a typhoon would most likely hit around the 210th day after the arrival of spring based on the lunar calendar; they had to work backwards 210 days and plan when to seed, to transplant and to harvest. All these works needed collective team work that became one of the basic needs of a settlement.

Nara/Kyoto, Osaka, Edo/Tokyo

Urbanisation as such started in the 8th century in the newly formed permanent capitals. First it was Nara (AD 710) and then Kyoto (AD 794). Till then the Imperial Court used to build a new palace for almost each new generation of lineage.

Kyoto had topographical advantage; it was easy to defend and rich in water supply, both from the rivers and underground. Before the industrial revolution, the river was an important transportation axis. Rivers connected Kyoto to Biwa Lake to the north, leading to the Korean Peninsula through Wakasa Bay and to Osaka to the south, leading to western regions through Seto-uchi Inland Sea. Kyoto thus became the Imperial capital resided by Emperors from AD 794 until 1868, with two Shogun governments located in other cities (Kamakura 1192–1333 and Edo 1603–1868) and one in Kyoto (1336–1573).

The city was built in a rectangular form, 5.2 km by 7.4 km with 11 boulevards and 22 avenues running North-South and 13 boulevards and 26 avenues running East-West at regular intervals. The central boulevard as an axis running North-South (Suzaku Ohji) was 85-metre wide and as the East-West axis (Nijo Ohji) it was 50-metre wide. Other avenues were 12 metres wide and boulevards were between 24 to 36 metres wide. Two public markets were built, one in the eastern part and the other in the western part of the city. Population was around 150,000 when the city was built.[1]

---

[1] cf. <http://env.sc.niigata-u.ac.jp/~uda/udat/heiannkyo.pdf> accessed 15 July 2014.

Elements such as political power, defence, water, transportation hub and economic activities are also relevant in today's cities.

Edo (today's Tokyo) was another example of a city built by political authority. It was built by Lord Tokugawa, who later became Shogun and set up a Shogun government in Edo in the year 1603. The largest challenge facing the city then was how to control several rivers, especially the one nicknamed Unruly River for its frequent flood. The solution was to dig a manmade river eastward towards Tone River to change the course of Unruly River and let the river flow directly into the Pacific Ocean, instead of Edo Bay (today's Tokyo bay). The Shogun government at the same time used the flat topography of Edo region to build a network of canals for transportation. Some of them were buried in the 20th century to be used as roads (an unfortunate belief in automobile transportation), while some environment-friendly canals could still be used.

The Shogun's immense political power forced feudal lords (around 300 families) to keep their families in Edo but not in their respective fief. This meant that about 500,000 samurais lived in Edo, with an equivalent number of merchants and artisans who were also attracted to the city. The population growth necessitated hinterland for food production and agricultural development with newly reclaimed rice fields in nearby regions, thus raising farmers' income.

Feudal lords were obliged to stay in Edo every other year and had to make pompous procession every year between Edo and their own town. That resulted in a nationwide transportation system, including not only roads and cabotage but also hotels, restaurants and other service industries. Thus the city became the eastern hub of Japanese national economy, together with Osaka as the western hub. This double-hub national economy system encouraged the development of not only an effective transportation system but also banks, merchants and a nationwide production system led by wealthy bourgeoisie such as Sumitomo (in Osaka) and Mitsui (in Edo). They had their origin in the late 16th century and their descendants are still continuing their businesses as global enterprise groups today. The renowned Mitsukoshi Department Store in Nihon-bashi used to be the fief of the Mitsui Group in those days (it was offered to the Meiji government in exchange for the survival of the Mitsui Group which was regarded as pro-Shogun by the revolutionaries). The district where the Bank of Japan is now located used to be called Kinza, or Gold Guild where private banks flourished during the Edo period. In the academic sector, Edo also attracted promising human resources due to the distinctive prestige and academic authority of the Shogun Government Official University. There were schools built by feudal lords in their provinces but they were local. The common also sent their children to schools run by temples, samurai and the bourgeoisie because of the not only prevailing education mania but also the reality that education including mathematics did lead to many job opportunities.

These politico-economic activities in turn made Edo the world's first city with inhabitants exceeding one million. In fact, factors that attracted people to a city, such as a large population, various job opportunities, reputable schools, culture, theatre and other leisure facilities, fashion, wealth chances to gain wealth and transportation facilities, have been similar through human history. In other words, in the urban areas, these elements must be properly addressed to give the huge population decent life conditions.

Water, sanitation and transportation

Water and sanitation in Edo/Tokyo

One of the most important challenges for any city in the world is water and sanitation. Japanese cities are no exception.

In ancient times, a good balance between population (polluters) and mother nature (cleaner) had been maintained, and drinking water had been channelled from clean water well into each household. In Nara and Kyoto, the upper class also used water for sanitation. They diverted a stream from the nearby river into their mansions and built toilet above the open water pipe. Ordinary folks' sanitary requirements were a part of the recycling system. Waste was collected systemically and used as fertiliser in the farmland.

Edo had six main aqueducts such as the Koishikawa aqueduct (1590) which was built when the Tokugawa family started the construction of the Edo city. It was later enlarged to become Kanda aqueduct covering broader area. In 1654 the well-known 43 km-long Tamagawa aqueduct was constructed (from Hamuro village to Yotsuya in Edo), a part of which is still used by Tokyo Metropolitan Waterworks Bureau. Others were Honjo, Aoyama, Mita and Senkawa aqueducts, all of which were completed by 1696. Most of these aqueducts were built of stones and/or wood and led water to water-distributing wells from which water was drawn.[2]

As for sanitation, Edo had a unique recycling system. Excrement was collected systemically, sent to nearby regions by specialised boats and used as fertiliser. In comparison, at the time, Europe did not have a recycling system. People instead threw wastes onto the street from their windows. Paris is well known for its sewage tunnels network, but originally those tunnels were used simply for sewage collection before the sewage was dumped into the Seine River near Sevres. Thereafter in the 19th century people found Sevres to be too close to Paris to throw sewage so tunnels were extended to Argenteuil, a bit downstream; however the sewage remained untreated. Similar sewage collecting network to throw the wastes into river was first built in Mohenjo-Daro in India around 4,000 years ago. Those Indian sewage ducts were made of bricks.

Edo/Tokyo faced fatal challenges three times in its relatively short history in 1868, 1923 and 1945. In 1868 the Tokugawa Shogun government was taken over by very low class-samurai serving the feudal lords in the western region of Japan. They rebuilt the former Edo Castle into the new Imperial Palace and shifted the Emperor from Kyoto for legitimacy. The former Shogun was exiled to Shizuoka with all his powerful samurai mandarins. Samurai who served other feudal lords also returned to their fiefs. The population of Edo inevitably and sharply dropped, continuing its decline until the New Regime consolidated its power.

The newly installed government decided to establish a modern state system. The facelift started with the renaming of Edo as Tokyo which

[2] <https://www.waterworks.metro.tokyo.jp/eng/supply/index.html> accessed 15 July 2014.

means Capital of the East. A railway track was built in 1872 between Tokyo and Yokohama, its sea port. The Iwasaki family from one of the four revolution-winning Lords regions, Kohchi, established Mitsubishi and developed Tokyo's central business district with political connection. Modern urbanisation brought drastic changes made possible by the revolutionary change of the regime that uprooted not only the socio-political system as such but also denied the ancient regime's social, cultural and religious values.

The first modern sewage system in Tokyo (following the success in the Yokohama city) was built in 1884 in the Kanda area by the new government which had to face public health challenge after the outbreak of cholera in 1877. The city and the new state were still in confusion in that year; internal feud among the triumphant revolutionaries led to a civil war in the southern part of Kyushu Island, especially in Kagoshima prefecture.

The civil war ended with a victory for the majority faction of the central government which then proceeded to consolidate the new regime. With stability, the population grew, making the building of a sewage factory imperative. The Mikawashima Water Recycling Centre was thus constructed in 1922. Incidentally a part of the aforementioned sewage system in the Kanda area is still in use today.

Roads in Tokyo

The second challenge to Tokyo was the Kanto Great Earthquake that destroyed and burned down Tokyo and the Japanese national economy in 1923. Casualties and missing persons registered more than 105,000, and 60% of buildings and houses, including all ministries and most of factories, were burned down.

During the course of reconstruction, an ambitious plan to reshape Tokyo into a modern city with a broad and straight road network with green belt was proposed by the Mayor of Tokyo Shimpei Goto. However, the plan was blocked by the narrow-mindedness and greed of people including land owners and National Diet members, and only a sixth of the initially requested budget was eventually approved by the Diet. Tokyo missed a chance to reshape itself into a truly modern city.

A similar mistake was later repeated after Tokyo was bombed and totally destructed in 1945 during World War II.

One big difference between the city-planning of Nara/Kyoto and that of Edo at the moment of their construction was in their road system. The former took a rectangular shape and had a road system in which regular roads and large avenues/boulevards ran from an end of the city straight to another, with the Imperial Palace simply surrounded by walls located at the centre in the northern district. The latter was round in shape with the Edo Castle at the centre surrounded by many moats and roads running in circle as well as those radiating outward. The Tokugawas had the roads running in circle and narrow gates on those radiating outward so that outsiders could not attack with a large army. This basic structure of the Edo road network became a headache to Tokyo three centuries later.

After the population boom in the 1960s, national and metropolitan governments had no other options but to purchase land from private owners to expand and/or construct wider roads suitable for modern cities. As a result, Tokyo's roads surfaces today represent 16.3% of the urbanised 23 wards (101.786/622.99 km^2, total length of 11,870 km).[3]

Role of underground railway network and private suburban railway development

The two disasters that destroyed Tokyo in 1923 and 1945 had an unexpected result. City dwellers who lost their homes migrated to the suburbs.

The move was very much encouraged by private railway companies' business strategy of extending railway tracks towards suburbs and develop new residential areas with modern façade along their new railway tracks. Railway companies first gained profit by selling land and after people settled in they could subsequently gained from the fares charged to commuters. Denen-chofu, which is considered today

[3] <https://www.waterworks.metro.tokyo.jp/eng/supply/index.html> accessed 15 July 2014.

as one of the prime residential areas, was a typical case. The upper middle class rushed to buy their dream houses close to Tama River, surrounded by greens and efficient road networks radiating from a modern railway station nearby. The land was put on sale in 1921 and a new private railway opened in 1922, a year before the Great Kanto earthquake. There are many similar cases and this combination of new railway routes and residential area development continued until very recently.

These railway companies often own bus companies as well; those who are unable to buy land near to a train station could easily reach the station by bus. These residential projects were drivers for the population boom in Tokyo in the 1960s, a precursor to it surpassing the 10 million population mark when the Japanese economy reached an apex.

Tokyo had several inner-city railway lines and two underground railway lines before World War II. They complemented the dense web network of trams that served the population then. However, such a system could not serve the needs of a megacity with more than 10 million inhabitants. The result was the abolition of trams to give way to automobiles and the construction of a very dense underground public transportation system. The new underground railways were directly connected to the aforementioned suburban railways for the benefit of not only the commuters but also railway companies which enjoyed an increase in revenue through expanded passenger volume.

Today, a reverse trend could be observed with the ageing population and lower fertility. Grey couples whose children live apart from them have no demand for suburban houses with gardens anymore. They sell their houses and live in downsized condos in the city centre for the conveniences, the medical services and vibrancy they offer. For those who have no driving licence because of their age can also move around the city centre thanks to the dense underground railway network. This is not the perfect answer to the challenges of the greying Japanese society but it gives a partial answer through market mechanisms. Statistically, there were 2.8 million inhabitants who were 65 years old or older, representing 21.9% of the whole Tokyoites in 2013.

That means one out of 4.8 persons was an aged person. In comparison, the figures for 2003 were a respective 1.41 million and 12.1%, indicating that the number and percentage of aged citizens had doubled in 10 years.[4]

Extending Japanese experiences abroad

Facts about water and sanitation in the world

Water and sanitation are the main causes of meaningless deaths in many countries in the world. Every year, 580,000 children under the age of five die of diarrhea. Those who survive also suffer from undernutrition as diarrhea is largely caused by the lack of sanitation or by poor sanitation in poorly developed areas.

A news report from New Delhi Television Limited (NDTV) is the best indicator of the effects of poor sanitation:[5]

> '... So why was Vivek malnourished?
>
> It is a question being asked about children across India, where a long economic boom has done little to reduce the vast number of children who are malnourished and stunted, leaving them with mental and physical deficits that will haunt them their entire lives. Now, an emerging body of scientific studies suggest that Vivek and many of the 162 million other children under the age of five in the world who are malnourished are suffering less a lack of food than poor sanitation. ...'

In most countries, cities often have better access to sanitation, but not in India. The report added that '[n]o Indian city has a comprehensive waste treatment system and most Indian rivers are open sewers as a result'.

---

[4] <http://www.metro.tokyo.jp/INET/CHOUSA/2013/09/60n9d100.htm> accessed 15 July 2014.

[5] Gardiner Harris, 'Poor Sanitation in India May Afflict Well-Fed Children With Malnutrition, *The New York Times*, 15 July 2014, <http://www.ndtv.com/article/india/poor-sanitation-in-india-may-afflict-well-fed-children-with-malnutrition-558673> accessed 15 July 2014.

In cognisant of the importance of sanitation, in 2006, Japan proposed to the United Nations to declare the year of 2008 as 'The International Year of Sanitation'. The proposal was based on the Recommendation by UN Secretary General's Advisory Board on Water and Sanitation chaired by Japan's late Prime Minister Ryutaro Hashimoto and adopted by the General Assembly in December 2006. 'The goal is to raise awareness and to accelerate progress towards the Millennium Development Goals (MDGs) target to reduce by half the proportion of the 2.6 billion people without access to basic sanitation by 2015.'[6] Sanitation was added to the MDGs only in 2001 at the Johannesburg World Summit on Sustainable Development. The targets set have yet to be met.

The lack of clean water access has drawn attention, but not the lack of sanitation access, one of the basic needs of daily life, hygiene, health, life, dignity and education. In fact, the lack of sanitation access is one of the main reasons girls cannot continue or complete primary education in many countries, an often neglected area in the discussion on urbanisation.

Japan has attempted to extend her experience of clean water and sanitation access in both urban and rural areas to the developing world. It is the world's leading donor in the water and sanitation sectors with the aim of helping developing countries avoid the same mistake that it had made in the 1950s and 1960s. In the past, the Japanese people concentrated their time, resources and energy to reconstructing the nation from ashes after the World War II destruction. With the advancement of technologies, affordable devices are easily available today to keep the water clean in an environment-friendly way, especially in water and sanitation.

Japan had succeeded in rebuilding its nation and in harmony with the international community. In 1964 it accepted Article 8 of the International Monetary Fund to liberalise its foreign exchange, joined the OECD to harmonise economic policy with industrialised countries and hosted the Olympic Games. Its bullet train, Shinkansen, started commercial operation in the same year and French Le Monde journalist

---

[6] <http://esa.un.org/iys/> accessed 15 July 2014.

sang praises of its achievements in a book titled 'Japon, le troisième Grand' a couple of years later. These achievements however were not attained in harmony with mother nature.

The Minamata tragedy, the leakage of mercury from an upstream chemical factory, killed many fishermen and their families. So did the spread of the 'Ouch-ouch disease', a result of cadmium from a mine, which broke the bones of mainly female farmers in the Jintsu-gawa region.

In Tokyo, the poor sewage network and inefficient water recycling factories could not meet the demands of the population boom and the very rapid 'economic miracle'. Tokyoites realised the severity of the issue when Summer Firework Festival of Sumida River in the city centre of Edo/Tokyo, a tradition which began in year 1733, had to be cancelled in 1961. Though the official reason given was the worsening traffic jam around the Sumida River on the evening of firework where tens of thousands would congregate for the event, it was widely believed that heavy pollution of the river was the cause, resulting in the extinction of the much loved sweetfish in the river. And the Sumida River pollution was not an isolated case.

Negative public opinion forced the government to promulgate a series of new environment preservation laws and to speed up construction of sewage networks and water-recycling factories.

The process proved to be long and tedious. It took 17 years before the river could regain its cleanliness, and the fishing industry and the Sumida River Summer Firework Festival to resume. Tokyo today has one of the cleanest air and river/bay environment among the megacities of the world.

Success story in Phnom Penh

Phnom Penh is one of the few cities in ASEAN where people can drink water straight from the tap. In 1993, only about 20% of Phnom Penh was connected to water-distribution pipes that provided water service of between 8 and 10 hours a day. Today, 90% of Phnom Penh enjoys 24-hour water service with only 6% water leakage, a top class in the world. It must also be noted that 99.9% of users of water do pay for the water supply. The success story of Phnom Penh Water Service Authority was called a miracle, winning awards including ADB Water Prize (2004), Ramon Magsaysay Award (2006), Stockholm Industry Water Award (2010), JICA Recognition Award (2012) and Diamond Eye Award for Quality Commitment and Excellence (2014).

Phum Prek Water Purification Plant in the capital was constructed using Japanese official development assistance based on the master plan for Phnom Penh water supply drafted in 1993. The success was the result of the good teamwork between Cambodian and Japanese experts and engineers. Kita-Kyushu City Water Bureau had dispatched water engineers since the beginning of the project and drew plans and support human resource development of Cambodian counterparts. Kitakyushu engineers have been stationed in the plant and worked together with Cambodian experts and engineers; the protagonists were Cambodia's new generation. The Cambodian success was short of a miracle given the disastrous effect of the Pol Pot regime and human resources had to be nurtured almost from scratch to construct the basic infrastructure.

Contrary to the 'miracle' realised in clean water supply, Phnom Penh still faces a hard challenge in its sewage system both for sanitation and industry. There is no water recycling factory in Phnom Penh, and all industrial sewages are channelled to the nearby marsh and rivers. Sewage-related environmental laws have yet to be promulgated, and like many highly industrialised countries in the past, the general business mindset is not on environment preservation. Like Japan's Sumida River, fish stocks are fast disappearing from the Tonte Sab Lake.

Water is life

Urbanisation faces multifaceted challenges. Uneven wealth distribution is often the largest challenge in developing and emerging countries. Slums, garbage, school/education quality, hygiene, safety/crime, transportation and pollution are among the countless problems and challenges faced by emerging cities. Water/ sanitation and building of primary schools could well be the starting point.

Index

CPSIA information can be obtained at www.ICGtesting.com
Printed in the USA
BVOW06*1829210616

452916BV00004B/7/P